INTRODUCING
American Politics

Patrick Brogan and Chris Garratt

Edited by Richard Appignanesi

ICON BOOKS UK   TOTEM BOOKS USA

Published in the United Kingdom
in 1999 by Icon Books Ltd.,
Grange Road, Duxford,
Cambridge CB2 4QF
email: icon@mistral.co.uk
www.iconbooks.co.uk

Distributed in the UK, Europe,
Canada, South Africa and Asia by the
Penguin Group: Penguin Books Ltd.,
27 Wrights Lane, London W8 5TZ

Published in Australia in 1999
by Allen & Unwin Pty. Ltd.,
PO Box 8500, 9 Atchison Street,
St. Leonards NSW 2065

Published in the United States
in 1999 by Totem Books
Inquiries to: PO Box 223,
Canal Street Station,
New York, NY 10013

In the United States,
distributed to the trade by
National Book Network Inc.,
4720 Boston Way, Lanham,
Maryland 20706

Library of Congress Catalog
Card Number: 99–071118

Originating editor: Richard Appignanesi

2000 … And Then?

One issue in the United States will be settled by the election year 2000. The country will show whether it approved of the Republicans' decision to proceed with President Bill Clinton's impeachment. But a chronic predicament of American politics is unlikely to be resolved. For the past 30 years, the Democratic and Republican Parties have been in stalemate. Leadership has swung like a pendulum between the two, with neither party dominant for long. The one exception was Ronald Reagan's presidency (1981–89).

No president since then has enjoyed the sustained support of Congress. No party has managed to break the stalemate and impose its vision of government on the country.

The Republicans in Disarray

The Republican Party is deeply split. It has the moralists who insist that American society must be purged of the foul weeds of atheism, decadence and sin. There are traditional conservatives who want to reduce the role of government and cut taxes. And in the middle are a few moderates who might reach compromises on most issues with moderate Democrats.

The Democrats under Clinton were defined by their opposition to extremist Republicans. But the sad truth is that the leadership of both parties lost credibility. Both parties have been seriously weakened.

The Center Cannot Hold

The Democrats managed to shake off the public image they presented in the late 1960s and 70s of wild-eyed leftists, "tax-and-spend liberals", the party of militant feminism, homosexuality and excessive and unfair preferences for racial minorities. Bill Clinton succeeded in moving the party to the center. The great danger in this was a steep decline in political enthusiasm.

Is this perhaps what the country wants? To preserve the political balance and avoid all radical efforts to deal with the country's problems? Americans are very conservative people and dislike change – even when it is proposed by conservative politicians. The Constitution is designed to make radical changes very difficult. And it answers the country's mood.

The Constitution

The United States of America, unlike the old nations of Europe, has a formal date of birth and a birth-certificate. On 2 July 1776, elected representatives of 13 separate British colonies in North America voted for their independence from Britain at a convention in Philadelphia. They adopted the Declaration of Independence on 4 July.

That Declaration was not only the most important event in American history, but also stands as one of the most significant political events in world history. The principles of the Declaration and the Constitution, written 12 years later to set up a new government, are the founding charters of democratic government everywhere in the world.

The Slogan of 1776

The colonies had rebelled against the British government for imposing unpopular taxes on them, and also against the very idea of undemocratic governmental authority. The British government, far away in London, decided for itself how much to tax the colonies and how to spend the revenues. It carried out its decisions without consulting the colonists, let alone winning their consent. And this gave the colonists their most effective slogan in 1776 …

How To Set Up a Republic

Once they had taken the fateful decision to rebel, the Philadelphia Congress had to set up a government. They all agreed it was to be a republic. But there was a difficulty. There were no standard models for republican constitutions. In the 20th century, when most European monarchies were overthrown and scores of former colonies won their independence, they could use the American, French or Soviet models for their constitutions. The Americans had to decide without any precedents.

The Continental Congress first drew up Articles of Confederation – the first American Constitution. It was adopted in 1777.

It raised an army and put George Washington in command – and to this day, American presidents exercise, in theory, absolute authority over the armed forces as heirs to Washington.

The Confederation was enough to beat the British. But its inadequacies were quite obvious by the time the war was over in 1783. It was clear that something better was required if the states were to have any sort of federal government.

The Confederation lacked the authority to conduct foreign or trade policy or to settle the urgent question of its own and the states' debts left over from the war. The Confederate Congress convened a new Philadelphia convention in 1787 to write a new Constitution. The delegates' guiding principle was to prepare a legal framework that would put into practice the principles of the Declaration of Independence.

...WE HOLD THESE TRUTHS TO BE SELF-EVIDENT: THAT ALL MEN ARE CREATED EQUAL, THAT THEY ARE ENDOWED BY THEIR CREATOR WITH CERTAIN UNALIENABLE RIGHTS; THAT AMONG THESE ARE LIFE, LIBERTY AND THE PURSUIT OF HAPPINESS; THAT TO SECURE THESE RIGHTS, GOVERNMENTS ARE INSTITUTED AMONG MEN, DERIVING THEIR JUST POWERS FROM THE CONSENT OF THE GOVERNED...

"We, the People …"

These delegates who represented the states were careful of their privileges. But the principles of the Declaration prevailed. Delegates were bound to the view that government is the creation of the *citizens*, not the various states – it has no other existence.

The preamble to the Constitution begins with the words "We, the People of the United States …", and a great weight of history bears upon that simple phrase. Some prominent Americans opposed the Constitution because it curtailed the sovereignty of the states. We shall see what happened when 11 Southern states reaffirmed this opposition and seceded over slavery in 1861.

The preamble to the Constitution drawn up in 1787 reads: "We, the People of the United States, in order to form a more perfect Union, establish Justice, insure domestic Tranquility, provide for the common Defence, promote the general Welfare and secure the Blessings of Liberty to ourselves and our Posterity, do ordain and establish this Constitution of the United States of America."

American history and politics ever since has been about the attempt to live up to those high principles.

To proclaim that they were "the People", or that all men are created equal, was all very well, but a functioning constitution requires a more practical framework. To start with, the convention had to resolve the division of powers between the states and the *federal* government.

Defining the Separate Powers

There were 13 states in 1787: Connecticut, Delaware, Georgia, Maryland, Massachusetts, New Hampshire, New Jersey, New York, North and South Carolina, Pennsylvania, Rhode Island, Virginia. The states were less than nations but more than the provinces of Europe. The powers of federal and state governments are carefully shared out in the Constitution, with the courts left to determine disputes between the two.

Then the Constitution had to lay out the powers of the various branches of the new government.

The blueprint is at once very detailed and very vague.

It lists the powers of president, Congress and courts.

And ever since, the courts have been busy defining exactly what each particular phrase means.

The Constitution provides in great detail for the election of the president – but when that procedure was found to be unworkable, it was abandoned.

But there are also vague statements in the Constitution – for instance, that the federal government shall regulate inter-state commerce.

The founders would have been pleased that their successors found enough flexibility in the Constitution to adapt it to new problems and new situations. It is no mere relic of the 18th century. It is a document in whose intentional vagueness succeeding generations have found answers to problems its authors never dreamt of.

A System of Checks and Balances

The heart of the Constitution was a system of checks and balances. An efficient executive was obviously necessary "to provide for the common defence", among other things, but Americans did not want a powerful monarch, or substitute monarch, dominating the legislature and the courts.

We distrust government - be it a colonial governor or a far-away king in London ...

... or a president and Congress in Washington.

Distrust remained so strong that the executive's powers were hedged around with restrictions. This was the origin of the doctrine of the separation of powers, which provides that the *executive, legislative* and *judicial* functions of government are each independent of and equal to the others.

This is, as it was intended, a recipe for ineffectual, or at least very restricted, government.

The Separation of Powers

The doctrine of the separation of powers has limited presidents and Congress for two centuries, and has frequently frustrated the clear will of a majority of Americans. It remains as absolute now as ever. The other great separation, between the federal government in Washington and state governments, is less absolute. There has been a steady encroachment of federal power into local affairs.

The separation of powers broke down once in 1868, immediately after the Civil War, when Congress attempted, and nearly succeeded, in seizing permanent control of the executive and bending the judiciary to its wishes.

The most notorious failure of democratic principles in the Constitution of 1788 was that despite the ringing Declaration of 1776, all men were *not* equal.

Opponents of slavery assumed that it would wither away. In fact, with the development of the cotton industry, slavery expanded greatly in the early 19th century. The resulting dispute led to the most calamitous event in American history, the **Civil War** (1861–65).

The Two Houses

The Philadelphia convention had also to calm the fears of the small states that they would be dominated by the large ones. It was agreed from the start that there would be two houses in the legislature: a **House of Representatives** and a **Senate**.

Thus, while all men are created equal, this equality does not extend to their representation in the Senate. Alaska, with 400,000 citizens, has as many senators as California, with 35,000,000 citizens. Alaskans thus have almost 100 times the Senate representation of Californians.

This provision, obviously undemocratic, was "the great compromise" which allowed all 13 states to ratify the Constitution – and it is the one clause in that document which cannot be amended.

It was a huge concession. The undemocratic Senate is fully the equal of the democratic House. In fact, it is more powerful, because the Senate alone confirms presidential appointments and ratifies treaties.

All legislation and spending bills have to pass both houses.

But there is no limit at all on the Senate's ability to veto bills offered by the House.

Thus, a large majority of the democratic House can be thwarted by 51 senators, some or most of them representing very small states.

The other compromise needed to get the Constitution ratified by all the states was the Bill of Rights. This was not part of the original Constitution, but was added in a series of 10 amendments in 1791.

The Bill of Rights includes a number of essential protections – for instance, freedom of the press and of religion, and the right to fair trial – that have been the bedrock of American society ever since. It also includes some provisions so vague as to be meaningless ("excessive fines shall not be imposed"). They are generally ignored.

The Constitution has been amended 27 times – starting with the 10 amendments of the Bill of Rights in 1791. Some subsequent amendments have proved very important.

The courts subsequently decided that the amendment applied to corporations as well as to people, to the enormous benefit of American business. The amendment marked a great shift in powers from the states to the federal government.

The 18th amendment prohibited the sale of alcohol; and the 21st amendment canceled the 18th. No amendment has altered any of the fundamental principles of the original Constitution – except the 13th and 14th which outlawed slavery and discrimination against blacks, and the 19th which gave votes to women (1920). But even these fundamental changes were within the spirit of the Declaration of Independence.

The Constitution has lasted extraordinarily well, despite its various imperfections. The Supreme Court has managed to adapt it to the spirit of the age when that appeared necessary. Privacy, for instance, is now enshrined as a constitutional principle, though it is never mentioned in the original document. This means that laws prohibiting abortion are invalid.

On 20 January 1993, Bill Clinton took the same oath that George Washington swore on 30 April 1789, 10 weeks before the fall of the Bastille in Paris and the start of the French Revolution.

The State Governments

The United States is a federal union. This term means that the country is made up of separate states (originally 13, now 50) which have come together under a central government that deals with national issues. By contrast, in centralized states like Britain or France, the nation and its government come first. They may delegate authority to local bodies, but the central government is always supreme.

Each state has a governor elected for four years, a state assembly and senate. The Nebraska legislature alone has just one chamber (the unicameral system). All the other 49 states have both an assembly and a senate (bicameral).

There are primaries to choose party candidates too.

States raise their own taxes, which pay for education, local roads and other amenities. Most states rely chiefly on state income taxes, which are much less than federal income taxes, for their revenue. Some, however, have no income tax and depend on property and sales taxes.

Who's Got the Power?

There are great differences between the various state constitutions. In some, such as Texas, traditional suspicion of government has given the state governor few powers of his own. He depends for his authority on his popular support and his ability to cajole the assembly. In other states, such as New York, the governor has a great deal of power.

The result has been to strip the legislature of most of its powers. Californians' decisions are heavily influenced by television. Special interest advertising is often the deciding factor.

In cities, in states and in Washington, politics revolves around the struggle between councils, legislatures or Congress, on the one hand, and mayors, governors or presidents, on the other. At each level, action, such as the budget, is only possible when there is agreement between the two sides, the legislature and the executive. It is often very difficult to obtain, even when one party controls both.

The relative powers of Washington and the states were carefully set out in the Constitution. But over the years, the powers of the federal government, and of the president, have greatly expanded, often at the states' expense.

The process started with the Civil War and the abolition of slavery ...

And continued during the two world wars and the great economic depression of the 1930s.

But the president still has no direct authority over state or local governments.

The police and the school authorities, for example, answer to the mayor or the governor, not to the president. At the same time, his indirect authority is very great.

Federal Interventions

Over the years, Congress has enacted a great variety of rules and regulations concerning most aspects of life. It has set up federal agencies to enforce them, or has found ways of obliging the states to carry out federal rules, whether they like it or not.

The president retains one crucial authority to be exercised in extreme cases. Each state has a local militia, the National Guard, commanded by the governor. In an emergency, the president can take over the Guard by simple decree. In 1966, Governor George Wallace of Alabama "stood in the school-house door" surrounded by the Alabama National Guard.

The soldiers ordered Wallace to stand aside – and he obeyed. It was all very dramatic.

On a more routine level, the federal government now raises far more money from taxes than the states do, and Washington decides how to spend the money.

Starting in the 1980s, there has been a move to restore powers to the states, which has made some progress. But the great shift in power from the states to Washington that became most apparent under President Franklin D. Roosevelt (1933–45) has not been reversed.

The Federal Government

The federal government is divided into three branches: *executive,
legislative* and *judicial*. The president is elected every four years and is
the source of all the executive authority of the federal government under
the law. He is commander-in-chief of the armed forces, and directs the
activities of every one of the hundreds of thousands of federal civil
servants across the country.

The second branch of government is the legislature. Congress consists
of two houses: a House of Representatives elected every two years and
now comprising 435 members representing theoretically equal districts,
each with about 450,000 inhabitants; and the Senate, consisting of two
members from each of the 50 states. These members serve for six
years, and one third of them are elected every two years.

Puerto Rico and the District of Columbia

Puerto Rico, a large island in the northern Caribbean, was annexed from Spain in the war of 1898 – along with the Philippines which became independent in 1946. The Commonwealth of Puerto Rico enjoys all the advantages of statehood (governor, legislature, federal subsidies) and its citizens are citizens of the United States (and vote in American elections when they move to the mainland), but it is not represented in Congress, nor can it vote in presidential elections. The District of Columbia (DC) was set up under the Constitution for the national capital, Washington, and was administered by Congress until the 1960s. Its status is a flagrant and undemocratic anomaly. Its citizens have voted in presidential elections since 1964 but are not represented in Congress. Why haven't Puerto Rico and DC been made into states?

Adding new states requires a two-thirds vote in both houses of Congress and the approval of three-quarters of the existing states. There are quite enough Republican votes to block Puerto Rico and the District of Columbia indefinitely.

Struggles Between Congress and the President

Federal judges, cabinet officers, ambassadors, senior military officers and various other officials of the executive are nominated by the president, but they have to be confirmed in their appointments by the Senate.

This is one of that body's most important powers.

However large a majority I might win in a presidential election, the Senate can thwart me by opposing my appointments.

Over the years, there have been many battles between presidents and the Senate over various appointments, particularly judges and ambassadors. Under a quaint-sounding but very powerful tradition, the "courtesy of the Senate", the Senate will not vote to confirm a federal judge to his post if he is opposed by a senator from the state where the judge is to hold court.

Senior judgeships have remained vacant for years on end because one or two senators disliked a president's nominees. And there have been dramatic confrontations over appointments to the Supreme Court. The same goes for ambassadors.

Congress passes laws, including, most importantly, the **budget.**

Taxes are raised and government money is spent under the authority of Congress.

Congressional committees, for example the two armed services committees, keep a close eye on every department of government. They cannot give orders, but they have the power of the purse, so their wishes are treated as orders by the entire government.

The Power of the Purse

The president cannot spend a penny that has not been granted him (the term is "appropriated") by Congress. In 1973, after an agreement with North Vietnam ended American involvement in the Vietnam War, President Nixon continued to bomb Cambodia.

In 1995, in a dispute between President Clinton and Congress, the president vetoed a spending (appropriations) bill that he considered wasteful, and Congress refused to pass another. A large part of the federal government then closed down. Special arrangements were made for the armed forces, the FBI and other important departments, but everything else stopped until Congress relented and passed an appropriations bill that the president agreed to sign.

If Congress passes a bill that the president dislikes, he can veto it, and it dies unless both houses can find a two-thirds majority to override the veto. Since no party can produce a two-thirds majority very often, the veto is a potent weapon. Congress sometimes gets around the presidential veto by adding bills that the president opposes to important money bills, such as the Defense Department authorization bill.

It is a game of chicken that sometimes Congress wins, sometimes the president. In 1995, Congress lost. The public blamed the Republicans, and the crisis helped Clinton to win re-election in 1996.

Congress over the years has passed many amendments that the current president disliked (like the ban on bombing Cambodia). The threat of doing so, and the president's counter-threat to veto, lead to much behind-the-scenes negotiation and compromise.

The Judiciary

The third branch of the federal government is the judiciary. It is independent of both Congress and president and it exercises its powers with far fewer restrictions.

Most state judges serve fixed terms, usually six or nine years, and are then eligible to be re-elected or reappointed by the state's governor. Federal judges can only be removed by impeachment, a process so cumbersome that it has been used only a handful of times in two centuries.

Judicial Review

Early in its existence, in 1803, the Supreme Court ruled that the judiciary could decide which acts of Congress were constitutional. Those that were ruled unconstitutional were therefore invalid, a process known as judicial review. Congress and the president of the day, Thomas Jefferson, accepted this astonishing assertion of power, which has been unchallenged ever since.

The people may support, Congress may pass and the president may sign bills into law, but if five of the nine members of the Supreme Court find the act unconstitutional, they win. The act is struck down.

The Parties

Political parties have no place in the American Constitution. That document was drawn up by a group of gentlemen who had the lowest opinion of parties, and of what we would now consider democracy. They thought that parties would always be corrupt groups of people pursuing their own personal interests, instead of the general good.

The founding fathers' caution was all in vain. Parties sprang up within a decade of the Constitution coming into force in 1789. They have played the dominant role in American politics ever since. The idea of the "great and the good" conferring harmoniously in electoral colleges to choose a president broke down in the first contested presidential election in 1796. George Washington was elected virtually unopposed in the first two elections, 1788 and 1792.

Origins of the Two Parties: the Democrats

The electoral college remains, mummified and useless, like the Privy Council in Britain. The function it was designed for – winnowing out potential candidates for president – is now performed by the political parties. This is their chief function. A large body of law and practice regulates the process – all without amending the Constitution.

The Democratic Party was founded in the 1820s, though it claims its origins as far back as the 1790s. It dominated national politics until 1860. The Republican Party was founded in 1856.

Throughout the period from the Revolution to the Civil War, national parties were coalitions of regional interests, rather than the ideological parties they later became.

The Republicans

Opposing parties, which eventually produced the Republicans, were based in the North-East and the Mid-Atlantic states. They opposed slavery, and they wanted high tariffs to protect local industries from British imports, and a strong federal government to promote trade and commerce.

As the 19th century wore on, the question of slavery came to dominate everything else.

After winning the war, the Republican Party dominated national politics until the Great Depression began in 1929. Democrats then controlled Congress, with brief intervals, from 1930 until 1994. They also controlled the White House until the elections of 1952. The presidency has alternated between the two parties since then.

On the See-Saw

This alternation of the two parties has been so much a part of American experience for the past 140 years that most Americans cannot conceive that legitimate governments can operate in any other way.

There has been a steady shift away from both Democrats and Republicans in registrations (in many states, a majority may be registered as independents, neither the one thing nor the other), but on election day they will still vote for one of the two old parties.

Old Ways, New Ways

In years past, when party discipline was all-powerful, the leaders of the Democrats and the Republicans in the states usually decided which young men should be allowed to run for local office.

Such power comes with seniority in the committees that write legislation, especially spending bills. Until the 1970s, party leaders' power came from their authority to dole out committee assignments. The same leaders, gathered in smoke-filled rooms at the party conventions, would decide the nominee for president.

All this made for strong, cohesive parties, based more on power and influence than political ideology. There was very little of text-book democracy in the process. But the saving grace of the American experience is that the old ways never last very long. Party discipline used to fail at regular intervals. It broke down completely in the 1970s.

None of this applies any more. Since the two parties are so loose in doctrine and organization, there is little need for third parties. As Nixon and Reagan showed with the Republicans, and Clinton with the Democrats, either party can be shifted in quite new directions. The two parties nowadays are little more than labels that ambitious people select with an eye to winning elections on their own terms.

Internal Party Divisions

The Republicans are now the party of white superiority – if not white supremacy. President Clinton, a Democrat, won his greatest success by carrying out his promise "to end welfare as we know it", dismantling the legacies of the two great 20th century liberal Democratic presidents, Franklin Roosevelt and Lyndon Johnson.

It is difficult nowadays to speak of a party ideology on either side. One hot ideological issue is abortion.

The same contradictions can be found, in both parties, on all the major issues that separate them.

Democrats are divided between liberals and centrists. In earlier years, the party was even more deeply divided. Until the 1960s, the Southern states were solidly Democratic and deeply conservative and racist. Democrats therefore presented the paradox of a party of highly liberal presidents – Franklin Roosevelt, Truman, Kennedy and Johnson – and a Congressional party divided between flaming liberals from the North and the most hide-bound Southern conservatives who controlled the most important committees in both houses because of the seniority system.

There are still plenty of Democrats who want to reduce the inequality of incomes in the United States by taxing the rich to improve the lives of the poor. But there are also many loyal party members who want to balance the budget, cut taxes, and let the poor fend for themselves. Bill Clinton is one of them.

Reality and not Ideology

This ideological woolliness never strikes Americans as in any way odd. American parties, like America itself, remain profoundly unideological. Extremists will forever try to impose their views – be it on abortion, feminism, homosexuality, race, tax policy or the place of religion in society – but always come up against this bedrock refusal to be forced into rigid categories.

The point was strikingly illustrated in the Congress elected in 1994. Republicans won comfortable majorities in both houses, and that was a revolution. Democrats had controlled the House of Representatives all but four years since 1931, and the Senate all but ten.

Democrats had won the House in 1930 and the Senate in 1932.

Republicans won both houses in the 1946 mid-term elections and lost them again in 1948.

won both in 1952, lost both in 1954

won the Senate in 1980 (but not the House), only to lose it in 1986

The new Republican majority, under the leadership of the Speaker of the House, Newt Gingrich, issued a "Contract with America". This was a list of 10 bills that they promised to rush through Congress in 100 days as a first installment in remaking the government in their own very conservative image.

Within three years, conservative extremists were mounting a rebellion against Gingrich for failing to keep his promises. In the next Congress, elected in 1996, with a reduced Republican majority in the House, all pretense of conservative purity was abandoned and Republicans, like Democrats when they controlled the place, concentrated instead on arranging for federal money to be diverted to their constituents.

The Legacy of Slavery

American history, until modern times, was dominated by memories of the Revolution and of the Civil War, their causes and after-effects. The uplifting tradition of 1776, the triumph over tyranny and the establishment of constitutional government, has been balanced by the dark legacy of slavery and racism.

That legacy persists. After the Northern victory in 1865, Republicans tried to make the ex-slaves the equals of their white former owners. They failed completely and abandoned the effort.

Southern whites recovered control of the governments of the former rebel states and imposed "Jim Crow" laws.

They stripped us of most of our newly-acquired rights - including the right to vote.

Though they were no longer slaves, blacks were reduced to a state of utter dependence on, and inferiority to, the whites.

Rigid segregation was imposed throughout the South – including the capital, Washington – and lasted until the 1960s.

The schools were strictly separated and black schools were the poorest in the country. There were no blacks in the armed forces, except for a few units in the North that had white officers.

The Long Struggle Against Segregation

Blacks were never admitted to Southern cultural or social events.

Institutionalized racism became a part of American life in the South, as slavery had been before 1865. Large numbers of blacks moved North, where they lived in unofficially segregated "ghetto" areas, many of which later turned into slums.

America began the long road away from segregation in the 1940s and 50s, notably with the Supreme Court ruling in 1954 ("Brown v. Topeka, Kansas") that segregated schools were unconstitutional. The fight to give blacks equal civil rights reached its climax in the 1960s under the leadership of Martin Luther King.

It was the dominant domestic political issue for 20 years, and remains exceedingly important. The country is still grappling with the problem of equal rights, the legacy of slavery and Jim Crow.

The Republican Domination

The Republicans dominated national politics from 1865 until 1933. Their long success was more than just a legacy of their victory in the Civil War. They represented modern, industrial and commercial America. They were the future, and the Democrats were the past. Business supported the Republicans from the beginning, and still does.

The 11 states of the former rebel Confederacy, together with several border states, formed the "Solid South" that always voted Democratic.

But the pattern was broken in 1901. The president then was William McKinley, who has a strong claim to be the dullest president in American history. His vice-president was the flamboyant former governor of New York, Theodore Roosevelt.

Shortly after the inauguration in 1901, McKinley was shot – and a Republican king-maker exclaimed, "Now that damn' cowboy will be President of the United States!"

The new century thus began with a dramatic change in national politics. Teddy Roosevelt was the first president since Lincoln to use the powers of the office to the full.

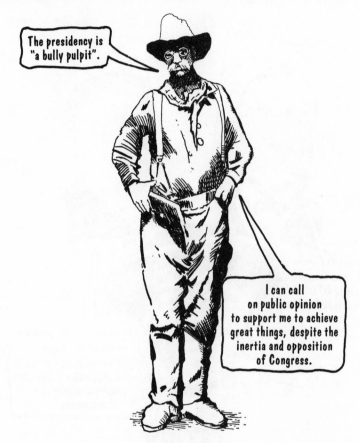

The presidency is "a bully pulpit".

I can call on public opinion to support me to achieve great things, despite the inertia and opposition of Congress.

He made the United States into a world power. He broke up the great monopolies, notably John D. Rockefeller's Standard Oil Corporation, established the national parks system and built the Panama Canal.

He was succeeded in the 1908 election by William Howard Taft, a very able, very dull, and very large Republican lawyer-politician. Yale University still cherishes a specially-reinforced chair built for Mr Taft.

A Democrat Becomes President

Taft did not follow Roosevelt's policies. After a bitter fight between the two in 1912, Roosevelt declared himself "as fit as a bull moose" and ran as an independent against Taft in that year's election. His Bull Moose Party offered a modern and progressive platform of reforms, most of which were later enacted by Democratic presidents.

Wilson was elected by 41.8% of the vote – the lowest percentage of a successful president since Lincoln in 1860, and the lowest of the 20th century. Roosevelt's career was over (Wilson refused to make him a general in World War I), and Taft later became chief justice of the Supreme Court.

Wilson carried on Roosevelt's work in reforming and modernizing the American government. He led the US into the war in 1917, just in time to defeat the last German offensive in the West in the spring of 1918. He was received as a conquering hero when he came to Europe to take part in the peace negotiations. He brought back the Treaty of Versailles (1919).

The Republicans in Congress repudiated Versailles and the League. They thought the League (a forerunner of the United Nations created after World War II) a gross infringement on American sovereignty. Treaties must be ratified in the Senate with a two-thirds majority – and there were quite enough Republicans to block Versailles.

Wilson's Campaign

Wilson set out on a train journey across the country, addressing huge rallies at every stop, urging support for the treaty. He was using the "bully pulpit" to the full.

American power must be used for good in the world ... to preserve the peace and prevent another World War.

He might have carried the day, but the strain was too much for him.

He suffered a stroke while campaigning in Colorado – and another worse stroke back in Washington.

For the last year of his term, Wilson was incommunicado in his bedroom in the White House. Government business was transacted through his wife, Edith, who carried messages into the sick-room and emerged, after a decent interval, with what she claimed were the president's decisions. She was thus the most powerful woman in American history.

Isolationism and Prohibition

The United States returned to normal as quickly as possible after the war. Americans retreated into isolationism, with disastrous consequences. If they had supported the European democracies, France and Britain, and democrats in Germany in the 1920s, World War II might have been avoided.

In 1920, the same Congress that rejected Versailles passed the 18th amendment to the Constitution, prohibiting the sale or use of alcohol.

The police were unable to stem the tide of illegal alcohol that poured into the country. The smugglers were called bootleggers, on the touching analogy of a man hiding a bottle in his pants. In fact, the smuggling was a vast commercial and criminal enterprise.

The Rise of Organized Crime

Bootlegging was directed by criminals who set up a loose alliance of gangs called *la cosa nostra*, "our thing". They were also known as the *Mafia* or the mob.

The best-known Mafia boss was Al Capone who ran the mob in Chicago.

The chief of the New York Mafia was "Lucky" Luciano, an immigrant from Sicily. Leaders of the mob families would meet periodically to settle disputes between them and to divide up the territory. Prohibition created a hugely profitable racketeering cartel that spread into drugs and became international.

Capone was caught on tax evasion charges and died in Alcatraz prison in San Francisco harbor. Luciano was jailed for running prostitutes, but used his Mafia connections to help the American wartime occupation of Sicily in 1943. In recognition for his services, he was released in 1946 and deported to Italy.

The mob infiltrate many trade unions and legitimate businesses.

We controlled the largest union in the country, the Teamsters Union, which represents truck-drivers and others.

In 1975 its leader, Jimmy Hoffa, disappeared. He was rubbed out by the mob. One story was that his body was disposed of in a meat-packing plant, another that he was cemented into the foundations of an office building. "Organized Crime", as it became known, is still a serious American and international problem, thanks to that "noble experiment", Prohibition.

Boom and Bust

In 1920, with President Wilson a recluse in the White House, the Republicans were certain they would win the election. There was a hot contest for the nomination. Warren Gamaliel Harding, Republican Senator from Ohio, won a landslide victory. He was one of the worst presidents in history. He died before the full corruption of his cronies was exposed. He was succeeded by his vice-president Calvin Coolidge of Vermont.

These two Republicans presided over the golden '20s and the long stock market boom. Wall Street flourished and Henry Ford sold his Model T in millions.

Coolidge retired in March 1929, leaving his successor, Herbert Hoover, to reap the whirlwind. Hoover, who made a fortune as an engineer, was later a distinguished public servant and secretary of commerce. He soon regretted what he said in his inaugural speech.

We in America are nearer the final triumph over poverty than ever before in the history of any land.

The stock market collapsed in October. The ensuing depression swept the world, brought Hitler to power in Germany, and led to World War II. Hoover proved quite incapable of comprehending the crisis, let alone dealing with it. Unemployment rose to over 20%. The stock market lost 89% of its value. The survival of the American democratic experiment itself seemed at risk.

Roosevelt and the New Deal

In 1932, Franklin Delano Roosevelt, governor of New York, won the Democratic nomination. He promised a "New Deal" for the American people, and easily defeated Hoover in November. At his inauguration in March 1933, he famously asserted …

It was one of the great turning points of American history, like Lincoln's election in 1860. The old order ended – the New Deal replaced it and defined American society and politics for the next 50 years.

"FDR" was by far the most important president of the 20th century. His policies dominated the country at least until Ronald Reagan's election in 1980. Much of his legacy has become a permanent part of American life. He gave America an interventionist, active government for the first time. And so it remains, despite all the Republicans' promises to rein it in.

I believe that government should help the poor and afflicted ... ensure that the children of the poor are as well educated as those of the rich ... and guarantee decent jobs, decent housing, and affordable health care to everyone.

These remain potent ideals, despite Republican and centrist Democratic efforts to repudiate them.

The First Hundred Days

When FDR took office in March 1933, the Great Depression had reached its depth and crisis point. American heavy industry, agriculture and service industries had virtually collapsed. Now, the banking system buckled under the strain. As the new president reached Washington, banks all across the country were closing down. Desperate customers battered at their doors to try to withdraw their savings.

FDR's first act was to order *all* the banks in the country closed.

FDR's first 100 days became legendary, and his policies rapidly produced their effect. Many presidents since 1933 have tried to set their mark on the country in their own first 100 days, without much success.

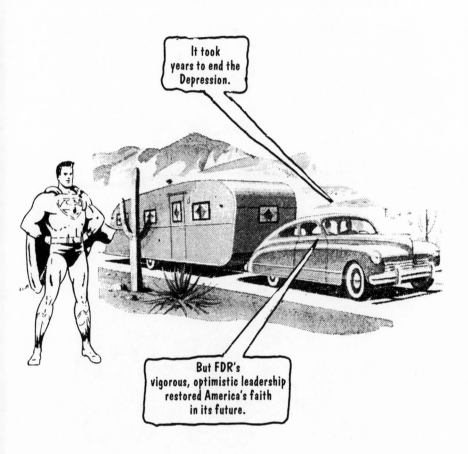

It was the classic demonstration of the power of the presidency in moments of crisis. The United States, burdened as it is with a Constitution that stands in the way of political decision-making, has been fortunate in discovering two of its greatest presidents, Lincoln and FDR, in its moments of greatest crisis.

FDR and World War II

Roosevelt's other great contribution was to prepare the country to enter World War II. When the war began in Europe, September 1939, Americans were mostly determined to stay clear. They had no wish to rescue Europe from its follies a second time. FDR saw that isolation and neutrality could not be sustained. He gave Britain every possible help, pushing the limits of his legal authority, in the dark days after Hitler's early victories. In September 1940, he sent Britain 50 old destroyers in exchange for leases of British bases in the West Indies. In March 1941, he pushed a "Lend-Lease" law through Congress.

It authorized me to supply all of the munitions and equipment that the British wanted ...

... on condition that they promised to return them after the war!

On this innocuous basis, he allowed the British to buy all the weapons they needed in the United States, on credit. The deluge of arms orders that poured in to American industry at last brought the Depression to an end and restored full employment.

While Congress debated Lend-Lease, convoys of freighters crossed the Atlantic, loaded to the limit with guns and munitions, and waited outside Liverpool until the bill was passed and the president had signed it. He also persuaded Congress to introduce conscription in peacetime for the first time in American history. The bill passed by one vote!

America therefore had the beginnings of her armed forces ready when Japan attacked Pearl Harbor in 1941.

In all this, he depended upon his own political success at home. He had won re-election in 1936 by the largest margin in history, and had then run for a third term in 1940, the first president to do so – and won again. In 1944 he was re-elected to a fourth term to finish the war.

Integration Begins

FDR's political coalition – the working classes across the country, the South, liberals everywhere, and poor farmers in the West – began to break up after the war as blacks demanded their rights and Northern Democrats rallied to their support. Harry Truman, an old-line Democrat from the border state of Missouri, succeeded FDR when he died in April 1945, just before the final victory in Europe.

The US armed forces obeyed their commander-in-chief, despite the large number of Southern whites in the officer corps. Another success of the times was in professional sport. In 1947, the Brooklyn Dodgers hired Jackie Robinson, the most outstanding black baseball player, and finally integrated the team. Before that, black athletes had played only in black teams against each other.

In 1948, at the Democratic convention in Chicago, liberals demanded that the party put a strong civil rights plank into its platform. Delegates from the Deep South walked out. Those states then voted for the governor of South Carolina, Strom Thurmond, on what they called the "Dixiecrat" ticket. (The South's nickname is "Dixie" after the Mason-Dixon line that defines the frontier on the map between North and South.) Thurmond carried several states.

50 years later, at the age of 96, I presided at the opening of Bill Clinton's impeachment trial before the Senate.

Truman's Victory

Truman was nominated by the Democrats. Thomas Dewey, the Republican candidate, was governor of New York and had run in 1944.

Truman pulled off the most famous upset in American political history. The day after the election he was photographed, grinning hugely, holding up a copy of the *Chicago Tribune*.

Truman's greatest achievements were in foreign affairs. He had authorized the use of the atom bomb against Japan in August 1945, abruptly ending the war in the Pacific, a decision hotly debated ever since. In 1948, as the Communists established Stalinist tyrannies in Eastern Europe, he persuaded Congress, which was controlled by the Republicans, to start the Marshall Plan (named after his secretary of state), which revived the economies of Western Europe and led, eventually, to the European Union.

In 1949, he established the North Atlantic Treaty Organization (NATO), and in 1950 sent the American army to the rescue when Communist North Korea invaded the South.

The McCarthy Years

Though he saved Europe, Truman lost China. That, at any rate, was what the Republicans claimed.

A general anti-communist paranoia developed in the United States, which Truman did not fight very effectively. This is known as the period of McCarthyism, after Senator Joseph McCarthy of Wisconsin, a drunken demagogue who raised up the demons of intolerance and suspicion by accusing the government of treason.

The Republicans, under a famous general, Dwight "Ike" Eisenhower, won the presidency in 1952, with a young senator from California, Richard Nixon, as vice-president. The Republicans won Congress again, but lost it two years later.

For the first couple of years of Ike's term, McCarthy was allowed to pursue his crusade against communists, socialists and liberals, poisoning public life and trampling on the liberties listed in the Constitution.

I chose Nixon because he had led the anti-communist witch-hunt as a member of the House UnAmerican Activities Committee.

The president allowed McCarthy to accuse the former secretary of state, Dean Acheson, and Eisenhower's own former boss, General George Marshall, of communism. In due course, however, McCarthy went too far. He accused the Army of being a nest of communists. The Senate at last found the courage to stand up to him and formally voted to censure him in 1954. The measure was proposed by Sam Ervin of North Carolina who presided over the Watergate hearings in 1973.

The Texas Connection

After the witch-hunt was over, Eisenhower, who was from Texas, developed close relations with the Democrats' leader in the Senate, Lyndon Johnson, and the Democratic leader in the House, Sam Rayburn, also both Texans. An era of unusual harmony between the two parties, and the great post-war economic boom, cast a glow of good feelings over the 1950s and early 60s.

Nixon was the Republican nominee in 1960, but was beaten by the Democratic candidate, Senator John F. Kennedy of Massachusetts. It was a very close election. Kennedy won because he had chosen Lyndon Johnson of Texas as vice-president.

Johnson controlled the electoral machinery in his home state. He made sure that Kennedy and he won with some very questionable votes from Democratic strongholds on the Mexican border. These votes were not counted until the tallies from the rest of the state had come in and showed a narrow Republican victory.

Well now, with these last votes we've got just enough to ensure a Democratic victory.

Even more dubious, Mayor Richard Daley of Chicago produced a last-minute horde of votes to carry Illinois for the Democrats. These two states made the difference. Nixon did not question the result, partly out of public-spiritedness, partly because the Republicans, too, had been stealing votes in southern Illinois and in Texas. They had made the mistake of announcing their results before the Democrats.

The Civil Rights Movement

In the 1960s, President Kennedy and his brother, the attorney-general Robert Kennedy, gave some cautious support to the civil rights movement which was by then gathering steam. Lyndon Johnson became president when Kennedy was killed in 1963, and was the ablest president since Roosevelt. Johnson made civil rights the centerpiece of his administration in domestic affairs.

I pushed through a Constitutional amendment that prohibited the setting of poll taxes as a condition for voting.

All the Southern states imposed taxes on voters, strictly collected from blacks who wanted to vote, which effectively deterred most of them from even trying.

Johnson pushed a series of civil rights laws through Congress, while admitting that their enactment would drive the South into the Republican Party. Indeed, the Deep South defected to the Republicans for the first time in history in 1964.

The long Democratic domination finally expired in the turbulent 60s, under the effects of the civil rights movement and opposition to the Vietnam War – though the party's control of Congress staggered on through the 1970s, thanks to the Watergate scandal.

YOUR INVITATION TO PARADISE!

I propose a "Great Society". The federal government will bring prosperity to every corner of the country and to all its citizens.

L.B.J.

Johnson's programs proved very expensive and not very effective. The majority of the population, who were neither poor, black, nor disadvantaged, objected to paying stiff taxes to support the poor and minorities.

The Goldwater Message

In the 1964 election, the Republicans put up a staunch conservative, Senator Barry Goldwater of Arizona. He offered "a choice, not an echo", meaning that the Republican Party proposed a complete break with Roosevelt's policies. He lost, decisively, not so much because his message was unpopular, as because the country was prosperous, the Kennedy legend was in full flower and Goldwater was thought capable of starting World War III in a moment of stupidity.

The Democrats ran a television commercial showing a pretty child running through a field of daisies. She stoops to pick a flower and starts counting off the petals ...

> One, two, three ...

A cold male voice overrides her in a countdown ...

> Three, two, one ...

The flowers, the child and the field are obliterated by a nuclear explosion.

It was one of the most effective political advertisements ever broadcast. It never mentioned the election, let alone Goldwater, but the message was clear enough. It only ran once (the Republicans howled in outrage), but that was enough. Goldwater went down to decisive defeat. All the same, when he carried the Deep South, it was a sign of things to come.

Prelude to Nixon

In the next election, in 1968, the governor of Alabama, George Wallace, one of the most prominent racists in the country, ran as an independent anti-liberal Democrat. At his inaugural as governor, he had proclaimed his policy.

Segregation today, segregation forever!

The era of the Solid South is over!

He carried four of the states that had voted for Goldwater.

Wallace also did well in the industrial North, pulling votes from the Democratic candidate, vice-president Hubert Humphrey. That too was a portent. The later successes of Nixon and Reagan were largely due to their ability to persuade Northern industrial voters that the Democrats were more concerned with blacks, people on welfare, and unpatriotic students than they were with the working classes.

Goldwater had shown the way and Nixon followed. He was a much more subtle politician than Goldwater, and much less conservative. He won the Republican nomination in 1968 and devised a "Southern strategy", moving the Party sharply right to please the conservative South and the suburbs, small towns and rural areas of the whole country.

The overriding theme of American politics by then was the Vietnam War. Kennedy and Johnson had led the country into it. By the time it was done, 55,000 Americans had been killed – and the war was lost.

All the same, it was a very close election, and Humphrey nearly pulled it off.

The New Generation

Nixon kept his word. He pulled American troops out of Vietnam. The final peace agreement was signed in Paris in January 1973, just after the 1972 election.

The Vietnam War was the most divisive conflict in American history since the Civil War. Many young men were vehemently opposed to it.

This was the same generation that rejected the conservative political, moral and musical tastes of the 1950s. They became known as the generation of "baby-boomers" who grew up after the Depression and World War II. The country's birth-rate had surged dramatically nine months after the soldiers returned from the war. Bill Clinton was born in the summer of 1946, for instance. And the high birth-rate continued through the 50s.

... and the Silent Majority

Their elders and the young conservatives, whom Nixon described as "the silent majority", detested their politics and posturing. Older, patriotic Americans, who had gone to war in 1941, saw no reason why the younger generation should not do the same. There was great tension in American society for the first time in a generation.

American moralizers believe in respect for authority and conventions. Liberals reject authority and conventions. The clash between the two views of society has persisted down the years.

The Rise and Fall of Richard Nixon

The Democrats nominated a noted liberal in 1972, Senator George McGovern. Nixon won one of the largest victories in history. He portrayed the Democrat as unpatriotic …

The Democrats hung on to Congress, but the tide was clearly running strongly against them. The Watergate scandal postponed the decisive Republican triumph.

The Watergate Scandal

Watergate is the key to American politics for the whole of the 1970s and 80s. Its ghost came back to haunt President Clinton in 1998. President Nixon, who had won a landslide election in November 1972, was forced to resign in disgrace in August 1974. He had used the great powers of the presidency to circumvent the laws, setting up a private police department answerable only to him, with authority to burgle, tap phones and perform many other illegal activities, all in pursuit of the president's enemies.

A group of them was arrested inside the Democratic National Committee headquarters in the Watergate building overlooking the Potomac River in Washington, June 1972. The slow unraveling of the story led eventually to Nixon – and to his resignation.

The Legacy of Watergate

Conservative Republicans, who could not condone Nixon's crimes, nevertheless claimed that he had been hounded from office by liberal Democrats. Those same liberals won a huge victory in the mid-term elections in 1974, three months after the president resigned – and the conservatives swore vengeance.

Relations between the two parties never recovered, and much of the bitter partisanship of the Clinton impeachment can be traced directly back to Watergate.

Nixon's vice-president, Spiro Agnew, had resigned in 1973 to escape trial for bribery. Nixon nominated a popular Republican congressman, Gerry Ford, as new vice-president, and Ford succeeded him when he resigned. Ford pardoned Nixon, a generous gesture that may have cost him the 1976 election.

One Term Carter

The country was still clearly moving to the right. In 1976, the Democratic candidate, Jimmy Carter of Georgia, barely won despite the Watergate stigma attached to the Republicans. He carried part of the deep South, his home region, a last case of historic loyalty to the party, and that proved enough to tip the victory.

He was an ineffective president, constantly thwarted by Congress, even though Democrats still controlled both houses.

Congressional Democrats, particularly in the House, have come to believe they rule by divine right.

Even the reforming class of 1974, swept into office by public revulsion against Watergate, acted as though they could govern the country without consulting the president – or anyone else.

Carter's Defeat

Carter's lugubrious personality displeased the electorate. The long economic recession provoked by the huge increase in the price of oil 1973–76 was laid at his door. Finally, in 1979, after a revolution in Iran overthrew the ruling Shah, a large group of American diplomats was imprisoned in Teheran. They were mistreated and humiliated, quite against international conventions.

Their long agony was also blamed on me ...

The Reagan Revolution

Carter was defeated in 1980 by the former governor of California, Ronald Reagan, who presented an optimistic, cheerful vision of the future – and carried the Senate for the Republicans for the first time in 28 years.

The "Reagan revolution" of the 1980s was less sweeping than the conservative changes introduced in Britain by Prime Minister Margaret Thatcher at the same time, because of the difficulty any president meets pushing his program through Congress. All the same, it represented a fundamental change in American politics. Conservatism triumphed, liberalism became a dirty word. After the resounding defeat of Walter Mondale, Carter's former vice-president, in the 1984 election, the country pronounced liberalism dead.

The Democratic Come-Back

Reagan's vice-president, George Bush, won the 1988 election.
Congress was still Democratic – the Republicans had lost the Senate in
the 1986 mid-term elections – and Bush failed to enact a conservative
agenda, but he did set the government on the way to eliminating the
budget deficits of the Reagan era.

George

> I was president
> when the Berlin Wall and
> the Eastern European Communist regimes
> collapsed - followed by the
> Soviet Union.

Republicans make the preposterous claim that Ronald Reagan was
responsible for the end of the Cold War. Bush also won a war in Iraq in
1991. None of this helped him in 1992. There was a recession, he was
blamed, and the Democrats won.

Bill Clinton was elected as a moderate Democrat but tried to enact some relatively liberal measures in his first two years. He failed and lost control of Congress in 1994. After that, he dropped liberalism, boasted that he was as tough on crime as anyone else, and promised "to end welfare as we know it". He presided over the dismantling of a large part of the welfare state set up by FDR.

But I promise to shore up two essential programs for the middle classes - Social Security and Medicare - which both help retired people.

The Republicans were still moving right, embracing the doctrines of the Christian Coalition and other extremists. Clinton, meanwhile, led the Democrats to the center. They did not like him for it.

The Lessons of Compromise

When Clinton's personal problems nearly overwhelmed him in 1998 – in the Lewinsky sex scandal – Congressional Democrats were notably slow in rushing to his defense. But his policies won elections, and even the last die-hard liberals could see that they must compromise if they were to win.

By contrast, die-hard Republicans drew the opposite lessons from their Congress victory in 1994. Then they failed to defeat Clinton in 1996 and lost seats in Congress – losing more in 1998.

We continue to argue that the party must move **farther** to the right.

Despite the president's continuing popularity, they insisted on impeaching him in the House and putting him on trial in the Senate – moves that, at the very least, endangered their hold on Congress.

The evangelical wing of the Republican Party, although it represented no more than 20% of the electorate at most, proved the most formidable part of the Republican coalition. Party leaders like Newt Gingrich had built themselves up as the voice of Christian conservatism.

Gingrich compromised with Clinton – but still lost elections. He resigned as party leader and Speaker of the House three days after the 1998 Congressional election.

The Electoral College

Under the Constitution written in 1787, presidents were to be chosen by groups of eminent citizens representing their states. Voters would select those electors in an election, and the electors would then gather in electoral colleges to choose the best candidate. The system is still in use – but voters choose the president, not the electoral college.

Each state has the same number of electors as it has members of Congress – two for its senators, and one or more for its representatives. The system was designed to favor small states, which have proportionately more electors than do big ones.

The notion that presidents should be chosen in two stages was abandoned in the first contested election in 1796. Voters in all the states voted for electoral candidates who represented one of the two contestants for the presidency – John Adams and Thomas Jefferson. Adams won.

T. JEFFERSON   JOHN ADAMS

The Magic Number 270

The Constitution has never been amended on this point. Americans still vote on the Tuesday after the first Monday in November in election year for electors, not for presidential candidates. The electors are, of course, committed to vote for particular candidates and gather in the electoral college (or rather colleges, one for each state and one for Washington) the following month. Then they ratify the popular choice – though from time to time a "faithless elector" votes for someone else. In theory, electors can vote for anyone they want.

There are now 100 senators and 435 representatives. So there are 535 electors, plus three for the District of Columbia. This means that the winner must get 270 electors. Since the early 19th century, all the states have provided that whatever candidate gets the most votes in November will get all that state's electors.

A narrow win in Vermont will give the victor its three electors. A narrow win in California will give him all that gigantic state's electors. Elections are decided in California, and a few other big states, for that obvious reason.

If no candidate gets those 270 electoral votes, the election goes to the House of Representatives. This has happened once, in 1824 (though the House also decided the results of the elections in 1800 and in 1876, when the electoral college results were in doubt).

In theory, it could happen again if a third party candidate won enough states. It might have happened in 1860, 1912 and 1968, when one of the main parties split and when third party candidates carried a number of states – or in 1992 when Ross Perot won 20% of the popular vote. However, he did not carry a single state, and therefore had no electoral votes.

Congressional Elections

Congressional elections show American democracy at its best – and worst. The national and local legislatures have gone to great lengths, in most places, to ensure that voting is fair and that the people's will is most accurately expressed.

Voters turn out every summer of election year to choose their party's candidate for the general election in November. Candidates are no longer imposed upon the electorate by party machines, gathered in smoke-filled rooms far from the glare of the cameras. Everything is open and above board and democratic – in theory.

The reality is rather different. There are 435 members of the House of Representatives, and their term is two years. In the 1998 Congressional elections, 94 members (55 Republicans and 39 Democrats) faced no major-party opponent. And by party calculation, no more than 40 of the remaining 335 seats presented any real choice. A total of only 17 changed hands. The Democrats gained 11 seats and lost six. In Florida, a major state with serious economic and social issues, there are 23 Representatives.

the City Beautiful
ORLANDO FLORIDA

In 18 of those districts, the incumbent faced no opponent from the opposite party.

14 of them, well over half Florida's Congressmen, faced no opposition at all.

FOR SUN-KISSED LIVING...
Coral Gables

Not even from the Flat Earth Society!

When nominations closed in the summer, they were declared elected, nem. con., "without opposition". Of the five races in which a Democrat and a Republican faced each other, in only one was the issue ever in doubt. The incumbent won easily.

No Contest Wins

This lack of opposition is not new. In the century after the Civil War, every elective office in the South was routinely won by the Democratic candidate. The only excitement came in the primaries. Lyndon Johnson's famous victory in Texas in 1948 was in the primary. That was the occasion that won him the nickname "Landslide Lyndon", after he won the primary by votes mostly stolen at the last moment. The general election in November was a formality.

The Democrats remain the overwhelming choice of black voters (one of the great ironies of American history), and of Hispanics. This gives them a solid base of support, at least in state-wide contests. They even made gains in 1998, picking up two governorships. They won one Southern Senate seat too – but lost another.

Gerrymandering

In many Southern states, there is a tacit deal between the two parties under which the states are carved up into safe Democratic and safe Republican districts. This is partly the result of one of the major achievements of the 1960s, the Voting Rights Act, which insists that minorities, meaning blacks, must be represented in Congress. This worthy objective has led to flagrant "gerrymandering" in many parts of the country. New York City "gerrymanders" to achieve "majority-minority" districts in which blacks can elect one of their own. The principle has now been extended to Hispanic voters.

The word "gerrymandering" dates back to the early 19th century, when a governor of Massachusetts, Elbridge Gerry, drew up the state's electoral districts to ensure his party's victory. A cartoonist published a map of Boston showing one such district resembling a salamander, and coined the word for the occasion.

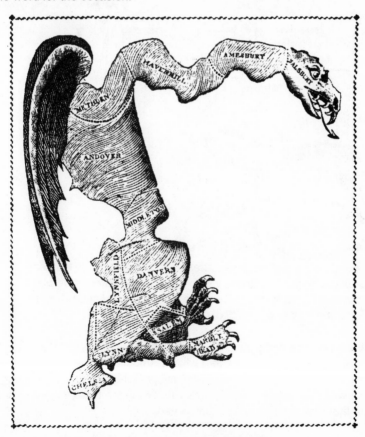

" O generation of Vipers ! who hath warned you of the wrath to come ?"

The Shape Matters

There is a national census every 10 years, and then the states are allocated a number of Representatives equal to their share of the population. Then the states redraw the boundaries of every district. In much of the South, the pact between the parties holds good. Republicans are only too glad to have all black voters in a few clearly delimited districts.

In Georgia, for instance, boundaries have been drawn to concentrate black voters in three districts, which therefore produce three black Democratic Congressmen. The state's other eight districts are all represented by white Republicans.

Critics have repeatedly gone to court in attempts to overturn the system. In Georgia, it means that white Democrats are all excluded from Congress – when 25 years ago, every Congressman from Georgia was a white Democrat. Republicans who live in the black districts also claim that they are forever unrepresented.

Throughout the nation, gerrymandering districts produces amazing shapes. Districts must be contiguous, so in one celebrated case, in North Carolina, widely separated black communities were drawn together into the same district by including a strip 100 yards wide along an interstate highway. The district was 150 miles long. Another district looked like a "Z".

In New York City, a Hispanic was guaranteed a seat in Congress by constructing a district that began north in the Bronx, wandered down the West Side of Manhattan, sometimes only a block wide, then cut across the width of the island to Brooklyn, continuing southeast for several miles. The district was about 55% Hispanic – and while there was never any doubt that a Democrat would win, whatever shape the district, a non-Hispanic stood no chance.

Tipping the Balance

One of the most-watched races in the 1998 election was for governor of California, which the Democrats won for the first time in 16 years. The Democrats already controlled both houses of the state legislature.

By winning the governorship, we put ourselves in charge of redistricting the state after the 2000 census.

California now has 52 members of Congress and will probably get four more after 2000.

GOVERNOR

In 1998, the Democrats won 29 and the Republicans 23 (the same as in 1996). The Democrats will redraw the districts in 2001, and might increase their vote in the House of Representatives by half a dozen, enough to tip the balance in a close national election – like those of 1996 and 1998.

Senate Elections

Senate races are not affected by census or party deals. All states always have two senators each. A third of the senators are elected every two years and serve six-year terms. The entire state votes for each of its senators in turn. So there is, again in theory, a real contest between the parties in Senate races.

But here again, some states are so committed to one party that the only contest is in the primary of the dominant party. Incumbents have to be singularly inept to lose their own party's nomination. In some cases, election to the Senate is a lifetime appointment.

In South Carolina, Strom Thurmond was re-elected in 1996 at the age of 94.

I had already served 41 years in the Senate – originally as a Democrat, then as a Republican.

There are dangers. In 1998, a Democrat won the governorship. If Mr Thurmond dies in office, the governor will appoint his successor – a Democrat.

Can a Third Party Ever Win?

The United States has enjoyed the two-party system, with Republicans and Democrats, ever since the Civil War. The two parties have proven indestructible. The case is made by the Republicans' survival in the 1930s when they were blamed for the Depression and ground down almost to vanishing point. Federal and state laws have been revised to incorporate the two-party system into the constitutional practices of the country.

In some jurisdictions, the one-party system is so deeply entrenched that a token opposition is provided by law. In New York City, the Republicans are allowed one member of the council, and in Washington there is a provision that one of the "at-large" city council seats must go to a candidate who is not a Democrat. An "at large" councilman is one that the entire city votes for, as opposed to councilmen who represent particular wards.

On a national level, the sharpest challenge to the two-party system came in 1912, when Teddy Roosevelt split the Republican Party, running as a Progressive. In 1992, an eccentric billionaire from Texas, Ross Perot, ran as a third party independent. He proved a much better candidate than anyone expected – and spent over $40 million on the race. The incumbent president, George Bush, was roundly attacked by Republican conservatives in the primaries.

Bush won the Republican nomination but was decisively beaten in the general election. The lesson of the Perot candidacy was that the American people were more ready to consider a third party candidate than their institutions allowed. Because of the first-past-the-post system of allocating electoral votes, Perot, despite winning 20% of the popular, got no electoral votes. Clinton was elected with 43% of the vote.

Third party candidates sometimes win election in state or congressional races. Vermont has elected a Socialist to its one Congressional seat for years, and occasionally independents win governorships. The latest was in 1998, in Minnesota, where a retired professional wrestler, Jesse Ventura, running on Ross Perot's Reform Party ticket, was elected governor.

Ventura won 37%. The Republican candidate won 34% and the Democrat, who had been expected to win easily, got only 28%. Most of Ventura's support came from dissatisfied Democrats – many of whom, a day later, were deeply astonished at what they had done. The defeated Democratic candidate was Hubert Humphrey III, son of the late vice-president and senator. It was as though Massachusetts had abandoned the Kennedys to vote for an independent bootlegger. Ventura won't be running for president in 2000!

Money Speaks!

America is a vast country with 260 million people. The challenge for would-be presidents is "How do I get all those millions to recognize my name?" The short answer is to obtain money, lots of it, for television advertising. But unless the candidate is a billionaire like Ross Perot who paid his own bills in 1992 and 1996, he can only raise large sums of money if he is already well-known.

Senators or governors can hope that most people who live in their own states know who they are, and members of the House of Representatives (congressmen) can hope to be recognized in their own districts – but that's barely a beginning. It helps a senator or governor to come from a big state (more people know him) but that's about it. How to get the rest of the country to pay attention?

Name Recognition

The one Democrat senator with name recognition throughout the country is Teddy Kennedy. Memory of his brothers, President John F. Kennedy (assassinated in 1963) and Senator Robert F. Kennedy (assassinated in 1968) is still strong, and Teddy has been a prominent liberal senator himself since 1962.

Newt Gingrich, Speaker of the House 1995–99, was the only really well-known congressman. He resigned from Congress after the Republicans did badly in the 1998 Congressional election. Then he divorced his wife to marry a woman who worked in his office (memories of Bill Clinton!) and his career appeared ended. Still, everyone remembers Newt. Other candidates have to scramble for attention.

A Woman President?

American party leaders do not rise through the ranks or emerge from the cabinet, like British prime ministers. Each must sell himself directly to the voters, first to get his party's nomination, then to beat the other party's man in the election. No woman has ever made a serious run for the presidency. Elizabeth Dole, known as Liddy, has offered herself to the Republicans this time. She has an advantage.

I am very well known. My husband was Republican candidate in 1996.

The odds are stacked high against her, and not just because she is a woman. She has never been elected to anything.

In 1984, the Democratic presidential candidate, Walter Mondale, bravely chose Geraldine Ferraro, a congresswoman from New York, as candidate for vice-president. She was not a very good candidate. The Democrats suffered a humiliating defeat, with Mondale carrying only one state and the District of Columbia.

The Golden Road to the White House

Ronald Reagan was a well-known actor who had a successful television show for ten years before he was elected governor of California.

There was a brief moment in 1995 when General Colin Powell, America's top general in the Persian Gulf War (1991), was touted as a new Eisenhower. But he declined to run in 1996. There are no other heroes or outstanding celebrities (though there are many billionaires) in a position to try their luck this time round.

The best way to reach the White House is to have been chosen as vice-president in an earlier election. The vice-presidency is not a powerful office but it gets a man recognized everywhere. He does not have to spend years introducing himself to every party official in the country and trying every trick of money and hype to get his face in front of television cameras and his name in the newspapers.

In the 13 elections since World War II, nine had a vice-president or former vice-president as candidate of one of the two parties. In 1968, both parties chose vice-presidents: the Democrat was Vice-President Hubert Humphrey and the Republican was former Vice-President Richard Nixon. In 1996, the Republicans nominated Bob Dole, who had been their vice-presidential candidate in 1976 (and lost).

Let's look at the 10 presidents since 1945. Five of them were former vice-presidents (Truman, Johnson, Nixon, Ford, Bush). The others were one general (Eisenhower), one senator (Kennedy) and three governors (Carter, Reagan and Clinton).

The Candidates in 2000

Vice-President Al Gore set out as favorite for the Democratic nomination in 2000. Bill Clinton has put all the power and influence of the White House behind him. This is always an immense help. In 1968, Vice-President Humphrey won the Democratic nomination thanks to President Lyndon Johnson's support – despite the violent opposition of the anti-Vietnam War movement. In 1988, Vice-President George Bush won the Republican nomination thanks to President Reagan's support – despite stiff opposition from the party's right wing.

Al Gore was senator from Tennessee when Bill Clinton chose him as Democratic candidate for vice-president in 1992.

The choice surprised people who had expected Clinton to "balance the ticket" by choosing a running mate who would add some other strength – someone from California, for instance, or the North-East.

Gore was born in Washington in 1948, son of a congressman who later became senator from Tennessee – Al Gore senior – who made sure that his son spent as much time as possible at home on the family farm in Tennessee. That was essential for a man hoping for a political career.

Al Gore senior was a noted liberal and lost his Senate seat in 1972 because of his opposition to the Vietnam War. Al junior was not so firmly opposed to the war as his father (or Bill Clinton) and went to Vietnam during his military service.

He's very smart, very competent and very dull. He makes jokes about his own lack of charisma. "Want to see me dance the macarena?" he will ask – and stand perfectly still for a few seconds.

Gore labors mightily to seem less wooden, more open. He can never hope to match Bill Clinton's ability to charm a crowd, but he has one advantage: his rivals are all equally dull.

He has devoted himself to environmental issues.

If I win the 2000 election, I will try to increase American efforts to cut greenhouse gases. I will support efforts to preserve the remaining wilderness against the encroaching suburbs.

After the Clinton disaster, it's necessary to say that (so far as we know) he has always been faithful to his wife, Tipper.

Clinton gave Gore various important jobs as vice-president. He led delegations to national and international conferences on the environment (including the Rio de Janeiro conference that produced a treaty to control global warming). He set up a task-force to reduce government bureaucracy (that was a very popular cause). And he supervised US relations with Russia.

Bill Bradley was a professional basketball player before entering politics. He was a successful, if rather dull, senator from New Jersey, and retired in 1994. Bradley is the most senior Democrat running for the party nomination against Vice-President Al Gore. Other prominent Democrats – including Congressman Dick Gephardt, the party's leader in the House and its most important active liberal – have admitted that Gore would beat them.

Bradley is another "centrist" moderate Democrat. His policies are indistinguishable from those of Bill Clinton and Al Gore.

My strongest card is that I am not Al Gore.

All the scandals of the Clinton years have tarnished the vice-president: not only sex but dubious campaign financing too. Bradley can say "My hands are clean" and offer himself as a new, honest Democrat who will follow the highly successful policies of the Clinton years without any of the Clinton sleaze or sordid fund-raising. Many Democrats support Bradley because they think that Gore would lose as a result of the Clinton stigma. Bradley is a real threat to the vice-president.

The Republican Contender

The front-runner for the Republican nomination is the governor of Texas, George Walker Bush, son of the former president. That's why he's favorite: it's a famous name.

I start off with the great advantage of being very well-known and popular in a big and rich state.

He was elected to a second term as governor in 1998 by a 70–30 vote. He has had no trouble at all in raising the $35 million or so needed to enter the 2000 primaries. The long list of rich, powerful and well-disposed Republicans who supported George Bush senior in his many campaigns are all ready and willing to support his son. Governor Bush therefore started out with a campaign organization in place in every state, while his rivals have had to battle to set up their own organizations, one state at a time, one supporter at a time.

The Bush family is from Connecticut. The governor's grandfather was senator from the state in the 1940s, and the president never shook off his image of a rich northeasterner. He was a Yale man, and behaved like one. Though he claimed that his home was in Texas, the only house he owned and his favorite residence was a large country house in Maine.

The future president went to war in 1941 and served in the Navy as a pilot.

He went to Yale after the war, and then moved to Texas with his wife, Barbara, to take a job in the oil business. His children were therefore born in Texas, and never let you forget it.

George Walker Bush is the eldest son. He had a not very distinguished business career running the Rangers football team, but was always tempted by politics. Texas was once a solidly Democratic state, but has been swinging Republican for the past 30 years. In 1994, the Republican party establishment needed a good candidate to run against the Democratic governor, Anne Richards. She was extremely popular and a very able campaigner. The party chose George Bush, chiefly on the strength of his name. He proved an adept campaigner.

He won re-election in 1998 in a landslide.

Bush is a firm conservative, but not a bigot. He has done much better than other Republicans among Spanish-speaking Texans, who are a very large community (Bush speaks Spanish), and among blacks, a constituency most Republican politicians ignore. He supports all the conservative social causes dear to the hearts of the extreme right.

However, he contrives to avoid the bitter, self-righteous animosity that seems to possess such conservatives as Newt Gingrich. He resembles Ronald Reagan. People like him even if they vote against him. He has admitted that he drank too much in his 20s – and gave up alcohol completely. He has all but admitted using cocaine in his youth, but as governor he supports laws imposing long sentences on all coke users. He agonized for months before announcing his candidacy, apparently fearing the sort of merciless scrutiny that Clinton has brought upon himself.

His younger brother, Jeb Bush, was elected governor of Florida in 1998. Jeb ran for the job and lost in 1994, partly because he presented himself as a hard, intolerant conservative.

This is MIAMI Beach

I learned from my defeat - and my brother's success - that moderate conservatives can win, while the dogmatic and self-righteous tend to defeat themselves.

If George Bush wins the 2000 election, Jeb Bush may play the sort of influential role in Washington that Robert Kennedy played (as attorney general) in John F. Kennedy's administration – and could conceivably run for the presidency himself at some later date, as Bobby Kennedy did.

Al Gore and George Bush are the favorites for their parties' nominations, though Bill Bradley is making a strong challenge to Gore. On the Republican side, the challengers are a few right-wing figures and Senator John McCain. One early casualty was former Vice-President Dan Quayle, who dropped out of the race in September 1999.

Quayle was George Bush's surprise choice for vice-president in 1988. Bush wanted a running-mate who was young, handsome and conservative.

It was meant to balance the ticket. But Quayle proved an extraordinarily inept candidate.

I never lived down the reputation of being out of my depth in high office.

He passed up the chance to run in 1996, when Bob Dole was favorite, and has tried to maintain his reputation as a staunch conservative during the Clinton years. He is an exception to the rule that former vice-presidents or vice-presidential candidates have the advantage.

Other Republican Contenders

Most of the potential Republican candidates are from the far right wing of the party, including leaders of the anti-abortion movement and various evangelical Christian movements. One exception is senator John McCain of Arizona, a former pilot who spent several years in a North Vietnamese prisoner-of-war camp. A staunch advocate of campaign finance reform, he would be well placed to win the nomination if Bush is brought down for some reason.

Another of Bush's rivals is Malcolm Forbes, a magazine publisher who inherited his media empire and his fortune from his grandfather – who came from the same Scottish village as media tycoon Rupert Murdoch's grandfather. Forbes believes that this sparse resumé gives him the qualifications for president.

And I'm rich enough to give Bush a run for it.

Forbes ran in 1996, advocating a flat tax of 15% to replace the graduated tax, and the exemption of capital gains from taxes. It is a program that appeals to millionaires. Since then, he has swung around to join social conservatives, who want to ban abortion.

How Much Money Do You Need?

All these candidates, Gore, Bush, Bradley, McCain, Forbes, have been actively preparing for their formal campaigns for the past year or much longer. This means they have been raising money.

"Money is the mother's milk of politics", said Tip O'Neill, Speaker of the House of Representatives in the 70s. Candidates for public office in the United States need enormous sums to campaign in primaries and in general elections.

... but lots of money goes on political consultants and polling organizations.

Most of the money goes on television advertising ...

We try to establish what issues will appeal to voters and how the candidates should present themselves.

In 1992, after she won election to the Senate in California, Barbara Boxer calculated that she needed to raise $10,000 every day for the next six years in order to run her primary and general election campaigns in 1998. In the event, the election proved even more expensive than she expected, and she spent well over $20 million in 1998. In that election, the two candidates in the New York Senate race spent $45 million between them.

The Billion Dollar Election

California is by far the most populous state and its elections are therefore exceedingly costly, and New York's media market is the country's most expensive. Candidates for House representatives throughout the country spend millions every two years, senators every six. Presidential elections are correspondingly expensive. In 1996, during the primary season, the government provided $30 million to each candidate who won his party's nomination (and lesser sums for those who dropped by the wayside). A further $70 million was given to each of the two party candidates in the presidential election itself. Ross Perot paid for his own campaign and declined government help. On top of that, the parties themselves and special interest groups spent hundreds of millions more. It was the first billion dollar election.

There are strict limits on how much an individual can contribute to a candidate ($1,000), or to a campaign ($5,000). The limits were imposed in 1975, after revelations of corruption in the Nixon campaign in 1972. Loopholes in the law were discovered immediately. Politicians and special interest groups formed Political Action Committees (PACs). An individual who has given the maximum to a party and to the candidates of his choice can then give $5,000 to a PAC.

There are theoretical restrictions on what a PAC may do with the money.

It can give no more than $5,000 to a candidate ...

But it can give to as many candidates as it likes - and there are hundreds of PACs.

Companies, lobbying groups and other special interests have their PACs send $5,000 a time to the PACs of important congressmen, who then pass on the money to their own supporters.

"Soft Money"

An even bigger loophole in the law is known as "soft money". Special interest groups can spend millions promoting a particular policy in a state or a district at election time, without mentioning any particular candidate and thus escaping all restrictions .

Soft money is the best kind, because it escapes all regulation. Every effort in Congress to reform the system in the 1990s was firmly shot down by the Republicans (to the secret delight of many Democrats).

A century ago, reformers denounced the notoriously corrupt Pennsylvania legislature as "the best that money can buy". They said the oil interests (John D. Rockefeller's Standard Oil Corporation) "can do anything they like to the legislature except refine it". These criticisms now increasingly apply to the national Congress. Special interests pour out huge contributions to favored congressmen, of both parties, despite all the laws, to buy their votes.

The most successful fund-raiser of all is always the incumbent president. Bill Clinton carried things to the extreme by selling nights in the White House to contributors for so many thousand dollars a time, making it the best-known (and most expensive) Bed and Breakfast establishment in the country.

Primaries

Most states hold party primaries in which voters choose the parties' candidates for various public offices. The dates are set by state law, and the two parties hold their primaries on the same day. When Americans register for the vote, they are given the choice of declaring their support for a party, or for none.

A voter registered for a party or for none is of course free to vote for any candidate he or she wants in the general election.

Before 1960, party presidential nominees were chosen by delegates to the conventions, and the delegates were chosen by conclaves of party activists and bosses in each state. Seven states, including New Hampshire, West Virginia and California, held primaries, and a number of others held state conventions at which delegates selected by party activists in each district chose delegates to the national conventions.

In 1960, Senator John F. Kennedy won all the primaries and all the conventions.

I built up a momentum that the party bosses who supported Senator Lyndon Johnson - could not stop.

Since then, every successful candidate has followed Kennedy's example. In 1968, Bobby Kennedy, competing with Vice-President Hubert Humphrey, won all the primaries except Oregon. He was shot in a San Francisco hotel kitchen after a California primary victory rally.

In 1976, Jimmy Carter put all his resources into the first primary, in New Hampshire.

When he won there, the victory allowed him to raise the money he needed for the next primaries. When he won again, and again, the money came pouring in – and though other candidates beat him in several of the late primaries, it was too late to stop him.

The great majority of states now have primaries. There are only a handful of convention states, including Iowa which opens the election year every February. The first primary is always New Hampshire. Other states have tried to get ahead of it or hold their primaries on the same day, but New Hampshire has always sworn to go first, even if it meant moving back to the previous year. Obstinacy has won.

Until 1992, no one was elected president who had not won his party's New Hampshire primary, so that contest always received saturation coverage in the media. That year, Bill Clinton lost in New Hampshire.

Despite this set-back, the New Hampshire primary remains one of the key events every election year.

Super Tuesday

In the 1980s, states envious of New Hampshire's prominence banded together. The South arranged to have a region-wide primary on the same day, 13 March 1984, and other states joined to produce one enormous nation-wide primary. The idea was that candidates would concentrate on the South, ignoring New Hampshire. They didn't.

The snowball effect still applied ...

Victory in the first primary brought in the money to pay for later campaigns.

In 1992, Clinton revived his campaign after his defeat in New Hampshire by winning the New York primary a month later, and used that as the lever to raise the money he needed to go on to victory. He was helped on the Southern Super Tuesday by the fact that he was a Southerner.

The primary pattern, well established by the 1980s, was finally broken by California. The most populous state had always held its primary in June. It was usually a meaningless exercise. The nominations had already been decided by then. In 1998, California abruptly moved its primary forward from June to March. In the 2000 election, the California primary will fall on 7 March, two weeks after New Hampshire.

New York, Massachusetts and Maryland will hold their primaries the same day, and Super Tuesday falls one week later when much of the South, including two other mega-states, Florida and Texas, will vote.

Seed Money for 2000

If the nominations for the two parties are not assured on 7 March, they will certainly be settled on Super Tuesday. The party system has now almost reached the stage of holding a national primary – a system that would hugely favor the richest candidates and exclude such candidates as Jimmy Carter or Bill Clinton. One expert calculates that any viable candidate must have at least $22 million in the bank by the end of 1999 to stand any chance at all in the first primaries.

The Convention

In theory, voters in primaries choose delegates to the party convention. However, the delegates are bound by law to vote for the candidate they represented in the primary, at least in the first ballots, so they have no power of decision in the convention.

The last party convention that actually chose the candidate was the Republican one in New York, 1940, which nominated a prominent businessman, Wendell Wilkie, to run against Roosevelt (he lost). The party leaders supported the governor of New York, Tom Dewey, but the galleries had been packed by Wilkie supporters who started chanting.

The movement swept the crowd, to the consternation of governor Dewey and his friends. Dewey was nominated at last in 1944, and again in 1948, losing both times.

Convention Drama

In all other elections since the 1930s, the candidates have been known before the conventions assembled. All the same, conventions can be exciting and important events.

The most dramatic was the Democratic convention in Chicago, 1968, at the height of the Vietnam War. Anti-war activists called for a vast demonstration. Mayor Richard Daley ordered the police to break it up, which they did with great violence. Tear-gas floated into the convention hall. Senator Abe Ribicoff of Connecticut denounced Daley in a speech to the convention.

Daley was so enraged that he ordered Ribicoff's microphone cut off. TV cameras filmed him gesturing to the managers by slashing his hand across his throat – and the microphone went dead.

The Campaign

Party conventions are held in July or August. Traditionally, the actual campaign begins in the first week in September, on Labor Day. In 1992, Clinton stole a march on the Republicans by starting his campaign immediately after the convention in New York.

They had huge press and television coverage. President Bush, who started his campaign in the traditional manner, a month later, never caught up.

In 1996, Clinton did it again. There were no surprises for the Democrats during the primary season (no one ran against Clinton), but the president used the large sums he had raised for the primaries to launch his presidential campaign, on television, over the summer.

Television campaigns are always aimed at specific markets.

Republicans would also waste their money in those states, since their victory there is assured. The object is to confirm those among their supporters who might not bother to vote, and to persuade doubtful voters.

Strategy

Campaign strategists try to guess what sections of the population might respond to what particular messages. Clinton, in both his races, was very successful with women, blacks and Hispanics. Bush in 1992 and Dole in 1996 did well in conservative Southern states.

Candidates fly around the country, attending rallies, dinners and fund-raisers in important states. In 1960, Vice-President Nixon promised to campaign in each of the 50 states.

No candidate has repeated his mistake. They all now concentrate on those states where their presence might affect the result.

Presidential elections are decided by votes in each of the 50 states and Washington, on a winner-take-all system in the electoral college. Whoever gets the most votes in California, for instance, gets all that huge state's 54 electoral college votes.

California voted for Republican candidates from 1968 to 1988. Both Nixon and Reagan were themselves Californians. It went Democratic in 1992 and voted for Clinton again in 1996.

Democrats usually expect to do well in New York, and Republicans in Texas and Florida. The other mega-states (Pennsylvania, Illinois, Michigan and Ohio) swing back and forth between the two parties – and presidential elections are very often decided there. Rocky Mountain states and the Great Plains usually vote Republican, as does most of the South. New England is mostly Democratic, and so are the mid-Atlantic states.

Televised Debates

The most important events of presidential elections are the televised debates between the candidates. Very many voters make up their minds on the strength of these performances.

There are now debates in primaries, too, and the result is that a candidate who performs well on television starts with a great advantage over his rivals. The first presidential debates were in 1960, between Richard Nixon and John F. Kennedy. Kennedy came off better.

Nixon never debated again.

The practice did not revive until the 1976 election, when President Ford and Jimmy Carter staged a debate during the presidential campaign.

It was an important and also farcical event. Just as the moderator was about to start the show, the telephone connection to the two speakers failed. Both remained stuck at their lecterns, like two dummies, for the next 40 minutes.

Once the problem was resolved, it became clear that Ford, who had spent his career in the House of Representatives, was not good on television. He also made the odd assertion that Poland was not a Communist country. Jimmy Carter was a preacher and came over as sincere, honest and trustworthy.

Ronald Reagan was an actor and did brilliantly in all his debates in 1980 and 1984.

Bush was not a very good debater – but better than the Democratic candidate, Michael Dukakis, in 1988. Bush won.

In 1988, the Democratic candidate for vice-president was Senator Lloyd Bentsen, a courtly Texan, much older and more experienced than Dan Quayle, the Republican candidate for vice-presidency. In their televised debate, Bentsen, in his lordly manner, suggested that Quayle was far too young for the job.

George Bush won the election and Quayle therefore became vice-president – but his political career never recovered from this exchange.

In 1992, there were three TV debates between Bush, Clinton and Ross Perot, running as an independent. Clinton did brilliantly, very much in the manner of a television talk-show host.

President Bush looked bored. He made the mistake of looking at his watch halfway through one debate. And he could not spell out his policies clearly. He lost badly.

No doubt the state of the economy was the most important reason, but Bush's failure in the television debates was also critically important.

Election Night

Elections are held on the Tuesday after the first Monday in November every four years. The 48 states of the continental US cover four time zones and individual states close their polls at different times. The television networks have taken a vow of silence.

As soon as the last polls close in the Eastern zone, at 9 pm, they start giving the results, with a fierce race between them to predict the result in each state – and to extrapolate to give a national result.

Time Warps

Chicago is an hour behind New York, Denver two hours and California three. Voters in all those places therefore know how the election is going in the East while they still have time to vote in their own states.

In 1980, it became apparent that Jimmy Carter was losing badly early in the evening.

The party never forgave him, claiming that many other races, for Congress or local office, were lost because Democrats, discouraged by their loss of the White House, stayed at home.

Party X Files

The Democrats did well in the 1998 mid-term elections. For the first time since 1934, the president's party picked up seats in Congress. The party was more or less united on the approach devised by Bill Clinton in 1992.

You've got to appeal to middle-class, moderate swing voters - but keep the loyalty and enthusiasm of the Democrats' core constituency among blacks, Hispanics and other minorities, labor, gays and women.

Republicans remained bitterly divided between evangelical Christians, who insisted on ever-more strident policies on abortion, prayer in schools and fundamentalist theology, and fiscal conservatives who cared little for abortion and so on, but were dedicated to cutting taxes and reducing the size of government. The party was also divided on the emotive issue of gun control.

Where Do We Go From Here?

There was a real danger that the Democrats would draw the wrong lesson for 1998 and conclude that they continue without any coherent and distinctive policies. If there is a recession by 2000, they could lose all their fair-weather friends of the 1990s.

George W. Bush, the governor of Texas, has the ability to hold the center without losing the support of the right wing, and showing blacks and Hispanics that he cares for their concerns. He won almost 70% in Texas in 1998 by playing down the sharp edges of Republican policies and appealing to the moderate center.

Clinton's campaign in 1992 had the slogan "It's the economy, stupid". He won because of the 1992 recession. He was re-elected in 1996 and did well in 1998 because the economy was booming.

Whoever is president when the stock market bubble bursts will be made to pay – as was George Bush in 1992.

Since 1968, the candidate on the right side of the economic cycle has always won the presidential election.

That said, the 2000 election will be decided by a TV campaign, both in the primaries and in the general election. That is why George W. Bush and Al Gore were the front-runners so early. They were the candidates who could raise the most money in advance.

One day, perhaps, real political issues will once again rise to the surface and there will be a real debate between sharply opposing political philosophies.

For the moment, there is no sign of any issue that would rouse enough passion to start a new party or unite and reanimate either of the two existing ones.

Impeaching the President

Impeaching the president was always described as the most dramatic power in the Constitution. Presidents serve for four years and cannot be dismissed from office for their failures, blunders or follies, however unpopular they may become. They can only be removed if they are proved to have committed what the Constitution calls "high crimes and misdemeanors". The phrase is not explained in the document. Both houses of Congress have to vote on the matter.

It takes a two-thirds majority in the Senate, meaning 67 of the 100 members, to convict the president.

The First Impeachment Attempt

Three presidents so far have faced impeachment. The first was Andrew
Johnson in 1868. He was vice-president, and took office in 1865
following Abraham Lincoln's assassination that year.

Johnson was accused of interfering with the social and racial revolution
that the North tried to impose on the South after the Civil War. A
majority in Congress considered the issue so important that it was
ready to upset one of the fundamental principles of the Constitution, the
"separation of powers", to get its way. Republicans were determined to
remove the president.

The Watergate Scandal

Richard Nixon, another Republican, was the second president threatened by impeachment, in 1974. Nixon was accused of subverting the laws and the Constitution by setting up a secret and illegal organization to spy on the opposition – and then covering up the crime when his operatives were caught during the 1972 election campaign burgling the Democratic party headquarters in the Watergate building in Washington. He denied the accusation in a famous TV broadcast in August 1973 …

He resigned before the House could vote. It was clear by then that he would lose in both houses.

Lying to the Public

Bill Clinton will go down in history as the president who had a steamy affair with a 22-year-old girl in his office – and lied about it. Congress put him on trial for perjury. The House of Representatives voted to impeach him – meaning it decided that he had a case to answer.

I was tried in the Senate - and they acquitted me!

The Johnson and Nixon impeachments were matters of very great importance. The Clinton affair was trivial by comparison. It was a sordid story of clandestine sexual encounters in windowless rooms and corridors in the White House. But there are two issues we should consider: Clinton lying under oath and the stubborn determination of the Republicans, led by the right wing, to see the president impeached at all costs.

The Jones and Whitewater Allegations

Clinton was often accused of sexual misbehavior. He usually denied all wrong-doing. In 1994, a former Arkansas state employee, Paula Corbin Jones, alleged that while Clinton was governor of Arkansas, he had made a vulgar sexual proposition to her. She claimed it amounted to sexual harassment.

Meanwhile, a special prosecutor, Kenneth Starr, had been investigating a land deal that Bill Clinton and his wife, Hillary, had entered in the 1980s.

It is alleged that Clinton used his powers as governor to help his partners in the property, known as Whitewater.

Starr, a right-wing Republican, extended his investigations to a number of other matters, but could not prove the Clintons guilty of any crime.

Paula Jones was supported and financed by people Hillary Clinton described as "a vast right-wing conspiracy against my husband". They persuaded the Supreme Court that a sitting president could be sued in a civil case, and Clinton was obliged to give a deposition, in January 1998, under oath. He denied Paula Jones's story. He was then asked about various other allegations of sexual misconduct – especially about Monica Lewinsky.

It was a trap set by the Jones lawyers. Lewinsky had worked as an intern at the White House before being moved to the Pentagon.

Tripp recorded dozens of phone conversations and turned the tapes over to the Jones lawyers – and then to Kenneth Starr.

Get Clinton!

In his January 1998 deposition, Clinton had denied an affair with Lewinsky. If he had known that she had prattled to Tripp, and that Tripp had told the lawyers, he would doubtless have confessed the truth.

Starr at last had hard evidence of the president's misdeeds. The details of the story promptly leaked to the media and an enormous scandal enveloped the president. Clinton denied in public that he had ever had an affair "with that woman, Monica Lewinsky".

Starr accumulated overwhelming evidence of the affair – including, finally, Lewinsky's own testimony. He had threatened her with jail if she refused to cooperate.

Public Opinion

In August 1998, Starr reported to the House of Representatives that Clinton had lied under oath. He said that was an impeachable offense. Clinton, faced with the collapse of his previous denials, admitted the lie but denied the perjury, a stand that few people found convincing. The Republicans then mounted the impeachment inquiry. They thought they could dispose of Clinton and increase their majority in Congress.

The booming economy helped the president. But standards of morality have changed. Adultery and other sexual games are no longer automatically condemned.

What is more, people thought the special prosecutor's investigations were an infringement on Clinton's privacy. If Starr could do that to the president, prosecutors could do it to anyone. Clinton's popularity was consistently in the 60s and even 70s percent.

The Republicans Self-Destruct

The most partisan of Republicans insisted on putting the matter to the vote. They were oblivious of the strength of public opinion. It almost lost them control of the House of Representatives in the mid-term elections in November 1998. The Democrats picked up five seats, the first time a sitting president's party had done so since 1934. Despite this evidence of the unpopularity of impeachment, the Republicans pressed ahead, even though this was a "lame-duck" session.

Clinton was impeached by the House on two counts – perjury and obstruction of justice – on 19 December 1998. It was a dramatic day. The speaker of the House, Newt Gingrich, had announced his resignation because of the party's losses in the election. Republicans chose as his successor Bob Livingston. Just before the impeachment vote, Livingston announced that he too was resigning.

Livingston's nemesis was Larry Flynt, America's leading pornographer, publisher of *Hustler* magazine, and self-proclaimed scourge of politicians' hypocrisy.

The Final Showdown

The drama of 19 December was compounded by the abrupt launching of an air attack on Iraq. Suspicious Republicans alleged it was an effort by the president to distract the public's attention. Republicans refused to let themselves be swayed from their purpose. The president was impeached by narrow party-line majorities.

Republicans in the House by then were like lemmings, intent on plunging over the cliff. Their colleagues in the Senate had more sense.

Party leaders went through the motions as quickly as possible, to the great indignation of House Republicans, who wanted a long trial with many witnesses, to do the president as much damage as possible.

Clinton was acquitted in the Senate after a three-week trial on 12 February 1999. The vote was 50-50 on obstruction. On the perjury charge, 45 Senators voted to convict, 55 to acquit. It wasn't even close.

The whole episode did the Republican Party a great deal of damage. It confirmed the general view that the party was controlled by puritan zealots. It also seriously weakened the doctrine of impeachment. It will be many years before a party with a majority in Congress tries to remove a president of the opposite party, whatever his misdeeds.

However, the episode also weakened the presidency, as well as the president. The affair stripped away almost every shred of privacy from the White House and demonstrated how vulnerable a president may be to law suits.

I am prepared to serve out the two remaining years of my term and deal with Congress that tried to remove me.

War in the Balkans

The impeachment of President Clinton failed, but his relations with Congress continued to be deeply troubled. Proof of this came barely a month after Clinton's acquittal in the Senate. On 24 March 1999, Nato launched a bombing campaign against Yugoslav Serbs led by President Slobodan Milosevic. These air strikes were justified by President Clinton, with the support of Britain and other Nato allies, on "humanitarian grounds".

Our aim is to prevent the massacre and expulsion of ethnic Albanians from the territory of Kosovo.

Kosovo belongs to Serbia.

Congress generally approved the effort to protect the Albanians, and salvage Nato, but the Republican majority in the House could not bring itself to support the president.

Republicans detested Clinton so much that when asked to vote in favor of the Kosovo operation in May, six weeks after the bombing began, they refused. And they also refused to invoke the War Powers Act.

The War Powers Act provides that presidents must get Congressional **approval** within 60 days of ordering the armed forces into action.

Yet, in spite of that, they voted not only to pay for military operations, but doubled the amount of money ($6.5 billion) the president had asked for.

Clinton Goes it Alone

So Clinton was in fact given a free hand to pursue the air war in Yugoslavia – but Congress would not say so. They also made it clear that they saw no need for any commitment of American ground troops. This was all a direct consequence of the bad blood between the president and the opposition.

The war in Yugoslavia is a dramatic illustration of the separation of powers. The president had lost all credibility with Congress but still, as commander-in-chief, he could order the full force of the American military into the first war in Europe since 1945.

The War Powers Act, which was meant to prevent such independent actions, was proved a dead-letter.

So, indeed, was that clause of the Constitution which gives Congress the power to declare war.

A judge in Arkansas could fine the president for his duplicity in Paula Jones's law suit – but nothing could stop the president from ordering the bombing of Belgrade!

Where Now?

America found itself ensnared in a complicated war scenario in a far-away place unknown to most Americans. Tony Blair, the Prime Minister of Britain, seemed especially keen to commit Nato ground troops to secure victory over President Milosevic in Kosovo. In the event, the air campaign proved enough. Milosevic surrendered and pulled his troops out of Kosovo, and Clinton claimed victory without having to send in the troops – or lose a single man.

Control of all three branches of government will be decided by the 2000 election. Either party may win the presidency or Congress, and because three of the nine members of the Supreme Court are likely to retire in the next few years, the new president will nominate their successors, which could swing the Court decisively either way. At the moment, it is split evenly between liberals and conservatives, with three swing votes in the middle.

But the stalemate between president and Congress, and between the parties, will not be resolved. Nor does it seem likely that either Democrats or Republicans will recover the unity, vision and dynamism that would give them a lasting victory. The political deadlock of the 1990s will continue into the next century.

With apologies to Thomas Nast.

Further Reading

Boorstin, Daniel. *The Americans* (3 vols.) (New York: Random House, 1958)

Brogan, D.W. *An Introduction to American Politics* (London: Hamish Hamilton, 1954)

Brogan, Hugh. *The Longman History of the United States* (London: Longman, 1999)

Rossiter, Clinton. *The First American Revolution* (New York: Harcourt, Brace, 1956)

Jahoda, Gloria. *The Trail of Tears: the Story of American Indian Removal, 1813–1955* (New York: Holt, Rinehart & Winston, 1976)

Lavender, David. *The Way to the Western Sea: Lewis and Clark Across the Continent* (New York: Harper & Row, 1989)

Morris, Richard. *The Forging of the Union, 1781–89* (New York: Harper & Row, 1987)

Foote, Shelby. *The Civil War* (3 vols.) (New York: Random House, 1958–74)

Foner, Eric. *Reconstruction: America's Unfinished Revolution* (New York: Harper & Row, 1988)

McPherson, James. *Battle Cry of Freedom: The Civil War Era* (London: Oxford University Press, 1988)

Oates, Stephen. *With Malice Toward None: The Life of Abraham Lincoln* (New York: Harper & Row, 1977)

Stampp, Kenneth. *The Peculiar Institution: Slavery in the Ante-Bellum South* (New York: Knopf, 1956)

Brown, Dee. *Bury My Heart at Wounded Knee: An American Indian History of the American West* (New York: Holt, Rinehart & Winston, 1970)

Hofstadter, Richard. *The Age of Reform, from Bryan to FDR, 1890–1940* (New York: Knopf, 1960)

Painter, Nell. *Standing at Armageddon: the United States 1877–1919* (New York: Norton, 1987)

Litwack, Leon. *Been in the Storm So Long: the Aftermath of Slavery* (New York: Vintage, 1979)

Livesay, Harold. *Andrew Carnegie and the Rise of Big Business* (New York: Addison-Wesley, 1975)

Link, Arthur. *Woodrow Wilson and the Progressive Era, 1910–1917* (New York: Harper & Row, 1954)

Galbraith, John Kenneth. *The Great Crash, 1929* (London: Penguin, 1955)

Brogan, D.W. *The Era of Franklin D. Roosevelt* (Newhaven: Yale University Press, 1950)

Leuchtenberg, William. *Franklin D. Roosevelt and the New Deal* (New York: Harpercollins, 1963)

McElvaine, Robert. *The Great Depression: America 1929–41* (New York: Times Books, 1984)

Allen, Frederick. *The Big Change: America Transforms Itself, 1900–50* (New York: Harper & Row, 1952)

Ferrell, Robert. *Harry S. Truman and the Modern American Presidency* (New York: Little, Brown, 1987)

Bloom, Jack. *Class, Race and the Civil Rights Movement* (Bloomington: Indiana University Press, 1987)

FitzGerald, Frances. *Fire in the Lake: The Vietnamese and the Americans in Vietnam* (New York: Vintage, 1972)

Smith, Hedrick. *The Power Game: How Washington Works* (New York: Random House, 1988)

A Chronology of Important Dates in American History

1492	12 October – Christopher Columbus makes first modern landing in New World, in the Bahamas.
1497	John Cabot makes first landing in North America, in Newfoundland.
1585	First English colony in New World, Roanoake, Virginia, founded by Sir Walter Raleigh. Fails after one year.
1587	Second Virginia colony. It also fails.
1607	First successful British colony, at Jamestown, Virginia.
1620	Pilgrims sail *Mayflower* to found first colony in New England, Massachusetts Bay.
1625	Dutch establish colony on Manhattan Island, calling it New Amsterdam.
1636	Harvard University founded.
1664	British capture New Amsterdam, renaming it New York.
1733	Georgia colony founded. British North America runs from Newfoundland to Georgia.
1756–63	Seven Years War in Europe (French and Indian War in North America). British capture Quebec and Florida. France cedes Louisiana to Spain.
1765	British parliament passes Stamp Act, first effort to impose substantial taxes on colonies to pay for western expansion and defense. Nine colonies send delegates to "Stamp Act Congress" to protest. They proclaim: "No Taxation Without Representation!"
1765–70	Increasing disputes between colonies and Britain on financing royal government in North America.
1770	British repeal most tax laws except tea tax (British merchants pay no tax, Americans pay large tax to import tea). Dispute subsides for three years.
1773	16 December – Boston tea party. Boston merchants dump British tea in the harbor.
1774	British parliament passes Coercive Acts to force Americans to obey British governors and pay taxes. Continental Congress assembles in Philadelphia, representing 12 colonies (Georgia and Canadian colonies stayed away).
1775	18 April – British army in Boston marches out to confiscate Massachusetts militias' arms. Militias warned by Paul Revere riding from Boston. British defeated in skirmishes at Concord and Lexington: "The Shot heard 'round the World!" August – George III proclaims the American colonies in a state of rebellion.
1776	4 July – Philadelphia convention votes Declaration of Independence. Thirteen colonies sign.
1775–83	War of Independence.
1779	French ally themselves with Americans.
1781	French navy defeats British and blockades British army at Yorktown in Virginia while Washington lays siege by land. British surrender 19 October.
1783	3 September – Treaty of Paris. Britain recognizes American independence from Atlantic to Mississippi. Florida returned to Spain.
1787	Constitutional convention meets in Philadelphia and draws up new constitution. Ratified by 11 states over the next year.
1789	4 March – new constitution comes into force. 30 April – George Washington sworn in as president in New York. Society of Tammany formed in New York, the first nucleus of the Democratic Party. John Adams, vice-president; Thomas Jefferson, secretary of state; Henry Knox, secretary of war; Alexander Hamilton, secretary of the Treasury. Supreme Court established.
1790	First national census: population 3.9 million, including 697,000 slaves.
1791	Vermont admitted to the union, first new state.
1792	Washington re-elected president.

1796	First contested presidential election. John Adams elected president, his rival Jefferson elected vice-president.
1800	Jefferson defeats Adams for president.
	Congress and president move from Philadelphia to the new capital, Washington.
	Census: 5.3 million (896,849 slaves).
	Napoleon forces Spain to return Louisiana (but not Florida) to France.
1801	Adams makes John Marshall chief justice, Jefferson becomes president, Aaron Burr vice-president.
	First foreign war, against Barbary pirates in Tripoli (now Libya).
1803	Marshall rules in *Marbury v. Madison* that Supreme Court can decide constitutionality of Acts of Congress.
	Louisiana Purchase. Jefferson buys New Orleans and Louisiana from France for $15 million: 828,000 square miles north of Texas and east of the Mississippi. He sends Lewis and Clark expedition to explore it. They reach Pacific in 1805 and claim whole territory for the US.
1804	Burr kills Hamilton in a duel. He remains vice-president.
1808	African slave trade declared illegal (in conjunction with Britain).
1812	US joins Napoleonic Wars, declares war on Britain. British navy blockades US ports. American attack on Canada fails.
1814	August – British burn Washington and attack Baltimore and New Orleans.
	December – Treaty of Ghent ends war.
1815	January – Andrew Jackson defeats British in Battle of New Orleans before news of peace crosses Atlantic.
	US Navy suppresses piracy on Barbary Coast in North Africa.
1817	Erie Canal linking Hudson river to Great Lakes begun, finished in 1825.
	Makes New York the main port in the US, and biggest city.
1819	Spain sells Florida to the US (but keeps Texas, California and south-west).
1820	Missouri Compromise: slavery not to be permitted in new states admitted north of Missouri.
1823	Monroe Doctrine: US states that European powers may not interfere in Central and South America.
1824	Political parties revive after long interval; John Quincy Adams defeats Jackson in questionable election.
1828	First election in which most states vote by popular vote. Jackson wins, establishes Democratic Party, proclaims "To the Victors belong the spoils".
1830	Census: 12.8 million.
	Indian Removal Act: all Indians to be driven west of the Mississippi.
1834	Whig Party formed (predecessor of Republicans).
1835	Seminole War: Seminoles of Florida deported to Oklahoma.
1836	Texan revolt against Mexico. Mexicans wipe out American rebels in Alamo of San Antonio (including Davy Crockett). Texans under Sam Houston defeat Mexicans under Santa Ana at Battle of San Jacinto: "Remember the Alamo!" Mexico recognizes Republic of Texas.
1837	Panic of '37 starts a depression that lasts until 1843 and leads to Whig victory in 1840 election.
1838	Cherokees deported from Georgia to Oklahoma along "Trail of Tears".
1840	Census: 17 million.
	First transatlantic steamship service, Liverpool–Boston.
1843	First wagon trails set out for Oregon.
1844	Sam Morse sends first telegraph message, Baltimore to Washington: "What hath God wrought!"
1845	Texas joins the Union: 28th state, 15th slave state.
1846	US makes war on Mexico.
1847	US army occupies Mexico City. In peace treaty, Mexico cedes New Mexico, Arizona, Colorado, Nevada, Utah and California.
1848	Gold discovered in Sutter's mill on the Sacramento River near San Francisco. Gold Rush begins at once.

1853	Commodore Perry of the US Navy sails into Yokohama Harbor, Japan. When he returns in 1854, Japan abandons isolation and opens to American (and European) trade.
1854	Democratic Senator Stephen Douglas proposes repeal of Missouri Compromise to admit Kansas as a slave state and Nebraska as a free state. Abolitionists oppose vociferously, found Republican Party.
1855–6	State of civil war in Kansas Territory: "Bleeding Kansas".
1857	Dred Scott decision by Supreme Court rules that slavery cannot be prohibited anywhere in the US, that the Missouri Compromise is unconstitutional.
1858	Douglas re-elected senator in Illinois after series of debates with Republican candidate, Abraham Lincoln. Lincoln says "A house divided cannot stand".
1860	Lincoln elected president.
1861	Southern states secede from the Union. 4 February – seceded states form the Confederate States of America, of which Jefferson Davis becomes president. 4 March – Lincoln becomes president. 12 April – South Carolina attacks and captures a federal base, Fort Sumter, in Charleston harbor. Lincoln proclaims the South in a state of insurrection and calls for volunteers to defend the union.
1861–5	Civil War.
1863	1 January – Lincoln issues Emancipation Proclamation, freeing slaves in rebel states (but not in Union states). 1–3 July – Battle of Gettysburg: in decisive battle of the war, Union army defeats Robert E. Lee, South's top commander.
1864	1 September – Union General Sherman captures Atlanta, Georgia, and marches to the sea.
1865	3 April – Union commander, Ulysses S. Grant, captures Confederate capital, Richmond, Virginia. 9 April – Lee surrenders to Grant at Appomattox, Virginia. Effective end of Civil War. 14 April – Lincoln shot. December – 13th Amendment to Constitution abolishes slavery.
1866	14th Amendment provides that "No state shall make or enforce any law which shall abridge the privileges or immunities of citizens of the United States; nor shall any state deprive any person of life, liberty or property without due process of law; nor deny to any person equal protection under the law", and gives federal government powers to enforce this article. US forces France to withdraw its army from Mexico. Emperor Maximilian shot in 1867. First transatlantic cable.
1867	Alaska bought from Russia for $7.2 million.
1868	Attempted impeachment of President Andrew Johnson. Senate fails to convict him by one vote. November – U.S. Grant elected president. December – President Johnson pardons all Confederate officials and officers, including Jefferson Davis.
1869	Wyoming gives votes to women in state elections. First transcontinental railroad completed, two sections meeting in Utah.
1870	John D. Rockefeller founds Standard Oil Company in Cleveland, Ohio.
1876	25 June – Battle of the Little Big Horn, Montana. General Custer and his cavalry wiped out by Sioux under Sitting Bull and Crazy Horse. November – Republican Rutherford B. Hayes defeated in presidential election, but wins anyway by corrupt maneuvers in House of Representatives. Alexander Graham Bell invents telephone.
1877	Crazy Horse surrenders; killed by US troops. Thomas Edison invents phonograph.
1879	Edison invents light bulb.
1880	Gold discovered in Alaska. New gold rush.

1881	President James Garfield shot.
1884	Grover Cleveland elected first Democratic president since 1856. He is defeated in 1888 but wins again in 1892.
	George Eastman, who had invented photographic film in 1880, invents roll film. Makes first Kodak in 1888.
1886	France presents Statue of Liberty to US.
1890	"Ghost Dance" Indian uprising; Sitting Bull killed.
	29 December – Battle of Wounded Knee, South Dakota; last episode in Indian wars. US declares the frontier closed.
	Census: 63 million.
1891	Edison and Eastman invent motion camera.
1893	Stock market crash leads to severe depression.
	Henry Ford starts making motor cars.
1896	Republican William McKinley elected president.
1898	Hawaii annexed.
	15 February – battleship USS *Maine* explodes in Havana harbor during an official visit: 260 sailors killed. US (notably the New York press) blame Spain (Cuba was still a Spanish colony).
	25 April – US declares war on Spain.
	1 May – US Navy defeats Spain in Philippines.
	1 July – US troops storm Spanish positions on San Juan Hill, near Havana, led by Col. Theodore (Teddy) Roosevelt and his "Rough Riders".
	December – Treaty of Paris: Spain cedes Philippines and Puerto Rico to US, gives Cuba independence.
1901	President McKinley shot; Teddy Roosevelt becomes president.
1903	US engineers' coup in Colombia's northern provinces, which proclaim the Republic of Panama. US signs Canal Treaty with the new state.
	Wisconsin holds first primary election.
1905	Roosevelt mediates end of Russo-Japanese war: Treaty of Portsmouth.
	Roosevelt awarded Nobel Peace Prize.
1906	18 April – San Francisco earthquake.
1908	General Motors founded.
1909	National Association for the Advancement of Colored People (NAACP) founded.
1912	New Mexico and Arizona admitted to Union as 47th and 48th states, the last territories of the "continental" US. Democrat Woodrow Wilson elected president when Republican party split.
1913	16th Amendment permits a federal income tax.
	Wilson holds first presidential press conference.
1914	Panama Canal opened.
	Wilson proclaims US neutrality in World War I.
1915	7 May – German U-boat sinks British liner *Lusitania* off Ireland: 128 Americans among 1,100 drowned.
1916	Wilson sends General "Black Jack" Pershing across the Mexican border in pursuit of guerrilla leader Pancho Villa.
1917	16 April – after Germans proclaim unrestricted submarine warfare, US declares war. Pershing leads 2 million men of the US Expeditionary Force to France.
1918	8 January – Wilson announces his "Fourteen Points" to end the war, including: "Open covenants of peace, openly arrived at"; freedom of navigation, in peace and war; free trade; arms reduction; "international guarantees of the political and economic independence and territorial integrity of the several Balkan states"; and a League of Nations.
	11 November – Armistice in Europe.
	December: Wilson sails to Europe for peace negotiations.
1919	28 June – Treaty of Versailles.
	18th Amendment bans sale and consumption of alcohol.
	September – Wilson campaigns for Treaty; suffers stroke in Colorado.

	December – Treaty defeated in Senate.

1920   20th Amendment gives votes to women.
Census: 105 million. For the first time, more Americans live in cities than in the country.

1921   First restrictions on immigration.

1925   Scopes trial in Tennessee: local teacher fined $100 for teaching Darwinism.

1927   20–21 May – Charles Lindbergh flies Atlantic from New York to Paris.

1929   14 February – St Valentine's Day Massacre in Chicago: Al Capone has six members of a rival gang shot.
29 October – Black Tuesday: collapse of Wall Street. In subsequent Depression, GNP drops by almost half.

1933   Franklin D. Roosevelt (FDR) becomes president, proclaiming: "We have nothing to fear but fear itself".

1934   Value of gold set at $35 an ounce.

1939   Albert Einstein writes to FDR, informing him of the possibility, and danger, of an atomic bomb.

1940   3 September – US sends 50 destroyers to Britain in exchange for bases in British possessions in Western Hemisphere.
16 September – first peace-time conscription in US history, passed Senate by one vote.
FDR elected for third time.

1941   January – FDR proclaims "Four Freedoms" – freedom of speech, freedom of religion, freedom from fear, freedom from want – as the guiding principles of America.
11 March – Lend-Lease Act allows US to send military supplies to Britain.
Manhattan Project (building the atomic bomb) started.
9–12 August – FDR and Winston Churchill meet on ships off Newfoundland and sign Atlantic Charter which proclaims war aims, including the formation of a United Nations (UN).
7 December – Japanese attack US Navy at Pearl Harbor, Hawaii.
8 December – US declares war on Japan.
11 December – Germany and Italy declare war on US.

1942   4–6 June – Battle of Midway: US Navy defeats Japanese fleet.
7 November – Allied landings in French North Africa.

1943   14 January – Casablanca Conference between FDR, Churchill and de Gaulle.
12 May – North African campaign ends with German surrender in Tunis.
10 July – Allied landings in Sicily.
3 September – Allies cross to Italian mainland.
9 September – US forces land in Salerno, near Naples.
22 September – Cairo Conference (FDR, Churchill, Chiang Kai-shek) followed by Teheran Conference (FDR, Churchill, Stalin). In Egypt, FDR meets King Ibn Saud of Saudi Arabia, forming alliance that has lasted ever since.

1944   4 June – Allies take Rome.
6 June – D-Day landings by Allies in northern France.
15 August – US invades south of France.
21 August – Dumbarton Oaks Conference in Washington sets plans for UN.
25 August – liberation of Paris.
7 November – FDR elected president for the fourth time; Harry S. Truman vice-president.
16 December – last German offensive, in Ardennes (Battle of the Bulge).

1945   7 February – General MacArthur takes Manila, Philippines.
February – Yalta Conference (FDR, Stalin, Churchill).
12 April – FDR dies; Truman becomes president.
24 April – UN opens in San Francisco.
7 May – Germany surrenders.
16 July – first A-bomb tested at Alamogordo, New Mexico.
6 August – A-bomb dropped on Hiroshima.
9 August – A-bomb dropped on Nagasaki.

14 August – Japan surrenders.

2 September – formal Japanese surrender aboard USS *Missouri* in Tokyo Bay.

1946 4 July – Philippines becomes independent.

1947 5 June – Secretary of State George Marshall announces his plan for restoring Europe.

5 July – armed forces united in new Department of Defense.

1948 Truman Doctrine: US guarantees Greece and Turkey against Communist subversion.

April – Berlin Airlift.

4 April – Nato treaty signed in Washington.

June – Selective Services Act: peace-time conscription resumed.

2 November – Truman wins election with 24.1 million votes, to 21.9 for Thomas Dewey (Republican).

California Congressman Richard M. Nixon, of House Committee on Un-American Activities (HUAC) accuses State Department official, Alger Hiss, of having spied for Soviet Union in 1930s.

1949 May – end of Berlin blockade.

October – Chinese Revolution. Republicans accuse Truman of "losing China".

1950 9 February – Senator Joe McCarthy of Wisconsin launches witch-hunt by asserting that he has a list of "205 card-carrying members of the Communist Party in the State Department".

25 June – Communist North Korea invades South.

Census: 150 million.

1951 22nd Amendment, limiting presidents to two terms.

4 April – Truman fires MacArthur as commander in Korea and Japan, for insubordination.

1952 1 November – first H-bomb tested.

4 November – Dwight D. Eisenhower elected president; Nixon vice-president.

1953 June – Julius and Ethel Rosenberg executed for spying for USSR.

July – armistice in Korea. US had lost 25,604 dead, 7,955 missing.

1954 May – Supreme Court rules in *Brown v. Board of Education of Topeka, Kansas* that racial segregation in schools, "separate but equal", is unconstitutional.

December – Senate condemns McCarthy.

1956 October – USSR suppresses insurrection in Hungary; Britain, France and Israel invade Egypt. Eisenhower uses economic pressure to end invasion.

1957 September – Eisenhower orders army to protect black students in Central High School, Little Rock, Arkansas.

October – *Sputnik I*, first orbiting space vehicle, launched by USSR.

1958 NASA founded.

1959 Alaska and Hawaii admitted to Union (last two states).

July – on official visit to USSR, Vice-President Nixon engages in "kitchen debate" with Nikita Khruschev, Soviet leader.

1960 November – John F. Kennedy (Democrat) elected president, Lyndon Johnson vice-president, defeating Richard Nixon (Republican).

1961 March – Establishment of the Peace Corps.

17 April – CIA-supported invasion of Cuba ends in fiasco at Bay of Pigs.

5 May – Alan Shephard first American in space.

25 May – Kennedy proposes to put a man on the moon by the end of the decade.

June – Kennedy meets Khruschev in Vienna.

August – USSR builds wall across Berlin to separate eastern and western zones.

December – first American soldier killed in action in Vietnam.

1962 February – John Glenn first American to orbit the earth.

22–28 October – USSR provokes missile crisis by installing nuclear missiles in Cuba. This was the most dangerous moment in the Cold War.

1963	April – Martin Luther King leads demonstration against racial discrimination in Birmingham, Alabama.
	June – Governor George Wallace "stands in the school-house door" to stop school desegregation in Alabama.
	August – King leads huge demonstration in Washington, proclaiming "I have a dream!"
	August – first nuclear Test-Ban Treaty.
	1 November – coup in South Vietnam leads to death of President Ngo Dinh Diem.
	22 November – President Kennedy assassinated in Dallas, Texas. Lyndon Johnson becomes president.
1964	California becomes most populous state (passing New York).
	Civil Rights Act outlaws most racial discrimination. Martin Luther King wins Nobel Peace Prize.
	2 August – after naval attack on US ships in Gulf of Tonkin, Congress passes "Tonkin Gulf Resolution", authorizing the president to take all necessary action in Vietnam. Vote is 416–0 in House, 88–2 in Senate.
	November – Johnson elected president in landslide over Barry Goldwater, but Goldwater carries the Deep South.
1965	March – Marines land in force in Da Nang, South Vietnam.
	"Operation Rolling Thunder", bombing campaign against North Vietnam, begins.
	Voting Rights Act ends Southern practice of excluding blacks. Black voters in Mississippi go from 22,000 in 1960 to 175,000 in 1966.
1966	First US bombs on Cambodia. By December, 385,000 US troops in Vietnam.
	December 1967: 485,000 troops; December 1968: 536,000.
1967	Johnson appoints Thurgood Marshall, first black Supreme Court justice.
	US population reaches 200 million.
	Race riots in Newark, New Jersey, and Detroit.
	October – March on Washington leads to huge protest against Vietnam War.
1968	30 January – Vietcong launch general offensive during Tet Festival.
	March – US troops massacre 200 Vietnamese civilians in My Lai.
	March – Senator Eugene McCarthy does well in New Hampshire primary.
	31 March – Johnson announces he will not run for re-election, and orders halt to bombing.
	4 April – Martin Luther King assassinated in Memphis, Tennessee.
	6 June – Robert Kennedy assassinated in San Francisco after winning the California Democratic presidential primary.
	May – peace talks with Vietnamese open in Paris.
	Most nuclear powers sign non-proliferation treaty.
	5 November – Richard Nixon elected president, Spiro Agnew vice-president.
1969	Nixon resumes full-scale bombing of Vietnam and Cambodia; begins withdrawal of US troops and "Vietnamization" of the war.
	20 July – first landing on the moon.
1970	US and South Vietnamese troops invade Cambodia to attack Vietcong.
	In protest demonstration in Kent State University, Ohio, four students killed by National Guard.
1971	June – secret Pentagon report on Vietnam published.
	August – US abandons gold standard
1972	February – Nixon visits China, meets Mao Zedong, settles future US-China relations; in May, he visits Moscow and concludes Anti-Ballistic Missile (ABM) Treaty.
	June – group of special government agents, "plumbers", arrested inside Democratic headquarters in Watergate building in Washington.
	Negotiations in Paris continue. In October, Nixon's national security adviser, Henry Kissinger, says "peace is at hand".
	November – Nixon re-elected.
	December – Christmas bombing of Hanoi.

1973	27 January – peace agreement signed in Paris.
	29 March – last US troops leave Vietnam.
	In *Roe v. Wade*, the Supreme Court rules that women have a constitutional right to have abortions.
	30 April – the president's lawyer, John Dean, reveals to prosecutors that the White House was behind Watergate. Nixon's two top aides, H.R. Haldeman and John Ehrlichman, resign. Dean fired.
	17 May – Senate Watergate Committee opens hearings. Special prosecutor (Archibald Cox) appointed to investigate president and his aides.
	10 October – Agnew resigns to escape indictment for taking bribes. Nixon selects Congressman Gerald Ford to succeed him.
	20 October – "Saturday Night Massacre": Nixon fires Cox, attorney-general Elliot Richardson and Richardson's deputy.
	23 October – Congress begins impeachment proceedings.
	24 October – all US armed forces put on alert ("Defense Condition Three") as USSR threatens to intervene in Middle East war.
1974	April – House Judiciary Committee subpoenas White House tapes. Nixon appeals to Supreme Court.
	9 May – House committee opens impeachment hearings.
	24 July – Supreme Court rules that president must hand over tapes.
	27–30 July – House Committee votes three articles of impeachment.
	8 August – Nixon resigns. Gerald Ford becomes president. Ford nominates Nelson Rockefeller to be vice-president.
	8 September – Ford pardons Nixon.
	OPEC begins progressive rise in oil price from $2.50 a barrel to nearly $40 by 1980.
1975.	Committees headed by Vice-President Rockefeller and Senator Frank Church reveal deepest secrets of CIA.
	17 April – Communist "Khmers Rouges" occupy Phnom Penh.
	29 April – Vietnamese Communists occupy Saigon.
1976	Fixed currency exchange rates abandoned.
	Jimmy Carter elected president.
1977	Treaty with Panama provides for canal to be handed over in stages to 2000.
1978	September – Camp David Conference: Carter mediates between Egypt and Israel, which sign peace treaty in 1979.
	November – nearly 1,000 members of US religious cult commit mass suicide in Jonestown, Guyana.
1979	US opens diplomatic relations with China for first time since 1949.
	4 November – US embassy in Teheran occupied; 52 diplomats held hostage.
1980	April – Mariel boat-lift from Cuba: over 100,000 people flee Cuba for the US, including many criminals.
	Secretary of State Cyrus Vance resigns after botched attempted rescue of Teheran hostages.
	November – Ronald Reagan defeats Carter in presidential election; George Bush vice-president. Republicans win Senate.
1981	20 January – hostages released from Teheran and Reagan sworn in at same time.
	Reagan names first woman Supreme Court justice, Sandra O'Connor.
1982	US sends Marines to Beirut to end Lebanese civil war.
	US becomes heavily involved in Central American civil wars.
1983	March – Reagan announces plans for missile defense system, "Star Wars".
	23 October – 241 Marines killed by truck bomb in Beirut.
	25 October – US occupies Grenada to counter coup.
	11 November – first US long-range missiles deployed in Britain and Italy.
1984	US completes withdrawal from Lebanon. CIA begins secret sale of weapons to Iran in exchange for help in releasing US hostages in Lebanon. Later, CIA uses profits of sales to help "contras" – right-wing rebels in Nicaragua.
1986	November – Republicans lose control of Senate.

	Iran-Contra affair revealed.
1987	New Soviet leader, Mikhail Gorbachev, visits Washington.
1988	21 December – 270 people killed over Lockerbie, Scotland, by bomb in Pan Am Flight 103.
	George Bush elected president; Dan Quayle vice-president.
1989	November – collapse of East German government; Berlin Wall torn down.
	Communist governments in Eastern Europe also fall.
	20 December – US occupies Panama to remove General Noriega.
1990	Iraq occupies Kuwait. Bush organizes international coalition to liberate it.
1991	Middle East War; "Operation Desert Storm" launched from Saudi Arabia 17 January; ground war begins 24 February, lasts 100 hours.
	First war in Yugoslavia, in Slovenia and Croatia. Bush refuses to intervene.
1992	War in Bosnia begins; US, EU, UN and Nato all refuse to intervene effectively.
	April – riots in Los Angeles after a jury acquits policemen of beating a black motorist, Rodney King.
	November – Bush defeated in election by Bill Clinton; Al Gore vice-president.
	December – Bush sends US troops to Somalia as part of a UN relief expedition. It turns into an attempt to end a civil war, and fails.
1993	February – bomb in World Trade Center, New York, kills five, wounds hundreds.
	19 April – FBI assault on a cult headquarters in Waco, Texas, kills over 80, including dozens of children.
	June – US launches missiles at government buildings in Baghdad.
	September – peace agreement between Israel and Palestinians signed at White House.
	October – 18 US soldiers killed in firefight in Somalia.
1994	March – last US troops withdrawn from Somalia.
	May – former state employee in Arkansas, Paula Corbin Jones, accuses President Clinton of sexual harassment in 1991, while he was governor of Arkansas.
	September – US occupies Haiti, to restore legitimate president and democratic system.
	November – Democrats lose control of both houses of Congress for first time since 1952.
1995	19 April – truck bomb at government building in Oklahoma City kills 168.
	September – Nato bombs Serbs in Bosnia.
	November – conference on Bosnia in Dayton, Ohio, leads to a peace agreement.
1996	November – Clinton and Gore re-elected. Republicans retain control of Congress, though with reduced majority in the House.
1997	March – 39 members of a religious cult, "Heaven's Gate", commit suicide in California, hoping to join a UFO behind the Hale-Bopp comet.
1998	January – press reveals details of a sexual affair between President Clinton and a White House intern, Monica Lewinsky.
	August – Clinton confesses to the affair.
	November – Democrats make gains in Congressional elections.
	December – House votes two articles of impeachment against President Clinton.
1999	January–February – Clinton tried in Senate and acquitted on both counts.
	March – Nato begins bombing Serbia.
	June – Serbian troops begin to pull out of Kosovo as Nato troops move in.

Presidents of the United States

George Washington	1789–97
John Adams	1797–1801
Thomas Jefferson	1801–09
James Madison	1809–17
James Monroe	1817–25
John Quincy Adams	1825–29
Andrew Jackson	1829–37
Martin Van Buren	1837–41
William Henry Harrison	1841
John Tyler	1841–45
James Knox Polk	1845–49
Zachary Taylor	1849–50
Millard Fillmore	1850–53
Franklin Pierce	1853–57
James Buchanan	1857–61
Abraham Lincoln	1861–65
Andrew Johnson	1865–69
Ulysses Simpson Grant	1869–77
Rutherford Birchard Hayes	1877–81
James Abram Garfield	1881
Chester Alan Arthur	1881–85
Grover Cleveland	1885–89
Benjamin Harrison	1889–93
Grover Cleveland	1893–97
William McKinley	1897–1901
Theodore Roosevelt	1901–09
William Howard Taft	1909–13
Woodrow Wilson	1913–21
Warren Gamaliel Harding	1921–23
Calvin Coolidge	1923–29
Herbert Clark Hoover	1929–33
Franklin Delano Roosevelt	1933–45
Harry S. Truman	1945–53
Dwight David Eisenhower	1953–61
John Fitzgerald Kennedy	1961–63
Lyndon Baines Johnson	1963–69
Richard Milhous Nixon	1969–74
Gerald Rudolph Ford	1974–77
James Earl Carter	1977–81
Ronald Wilson Reagan	1981–89
George Herbert Walker Bush	1989–93
William Jefferson Clinton	1993–

The Constitution

[The Constitution came into effect in 1789; the Bill of Rights (see p. 187) was approved in 1791.]

We the People of the United States, in Order to form a more perfect Union, establish Justice, insure domestic Tranquility, provide for the common defence, promote the general Welfare, and secure the Blessings of Liberty to ourselves and our Posterity, do ordain and establish this Constitution for the United States of America.

Article. I.

Section. 1. All legislative Powers herein granted shall be vested in a Congress of the United States, which shall consist of a Senate and House of Representatives.

Section. 2. The House of Representatives shall be composed of Members chosen every second Year by the People of the several States, and the Electors in each State shall have the Qualifications requisite for Electors of the most numerous Branch of the State Legislature.

No Person shall be a Representative who shall not have attained to the age of twenty five Years, and been seven Years a Citizen of the United States, and who shall not, when elected, be an Inhabitant of that State in which he shall be chosen.

Representatives and direct Taxes shall be apportioned among the several States which may be included within this Union, according to their respective Numbers, which shall be determined by adding to the whole Number of free Persons, including those bound to Service for a Term of Years, and excluding Indians not taxed, three fifths of all other Persons. The actual Enumeration shall be made within three Years after the first Meeting of the Congress of the United States, and within every subsequent Term of ten Years, in such Manner as they shall by Law direct. The Number of Representatives shall not exceed one for every thirty Thousand, but each State shall have at Least one Representative; and until such enumeration shall be made, the State of New Hampshire shall be entitled to chuse three, Massachusetts eight, Rhode-Island and Providence Plantations one, Connecticut five, New-York six, New Jersey four, Pennsylvania eight, Delaware one, Maryland six, Virginia ten, North Carolina five, South Carolina five, and Georgia three. When vacancies happen in the Representation from any State, the Executive Authority thereof shall issue Writs of Election to fill such Vacancies.

The House of Representatives shall chuse their Speaker and other Officers; and shall have the sole Power of Impeachment.

Section. 3. The Senate of the United States shall be composed of two Senators from each State, chosen by the Legislature thereof, for six Years; and each Senator shall have one Vote.

Immediately after they shall be assembled in Consequence of the first Election, they shall be divided as equally as may be into three Classes. The Seats of the Senators of the first Class shall be vacated at the Expiration of the second Year, of the second Class at the Expiration of the fourth Year, and of the third Class at the Expiration of the sixth Year, so that one third may be chosen every second Year; and if Vacancies happen by Resignation, or otherwise, during the Recess of the Legislature of any State, the Executive thereof may make temporary Appointments until the next Meeting of the Legislature, which shall then fill such Vacancies.

No Person shall be a Senator who shall not have attained to the Age of thirty Years, and been nine Years a Citizen of the United States, and who shall not, when elected, be an Inhabitant of that State for which he shall be chosen.

The Vice President of the United States shall be President of the Senate but shall have no Vote, unless they be equally divided.

The Senate shall chuse their other Officers, and also a President pro tempore, in the Absence of the Vice President, or when he shall exercise the Office of President of the United States.

The Senate shall have the sole Power to try all Impeachments. When sitting for that Purpose, they shall be on Oath or Affirmation. When the President of the United States is tried the Chief Justice shall preside: And no Person shall be convicted without the Concurrence of two thirds of the Members present.

Judgment in Cases of Impeachment shall not extend further than to removal from Office, and disqualification to hold and enjoy any Office of honor, Trust or Profit under the United States: but the Party convicted shall nevertheless be liable and subject to Indictment, Trial, Judgment and Punishment, according to Law.

Section. 4. The Times, Places and Manner of holding Elections for Senators and Representatives, shall be prescribed in each State by the Legislature thereof; but the Congress may at any time by Law make or alter such Regulations, except as to the Places of chusing Senators.

The Congress shall assemble at least once in every Year, and such Meeting shall be on the first Monday in December, unless they shall by Law appoint a different Day.

Section. 5. Each House shall be the Judge of the Elections, Returns and Qualifications of its own Members, and a Majority of each shall constitute a Quorum to do Business; but a smaller Number may adjourn from day to day, and may be authorized to compel the Attendance of absent Members, in such Manner, and under such Penalties as each House may provide.

Each House may determine the Rules of its Proceedings, punish its Members for disorderly Behaviour, and, with the Concurrence of two thirds, expel a Member.

Each House shall keep a Journal of its Proceedings, and from time to time publish the same, excepting such Parts as may in their Judgment require Secrecy; and the Yeas and Nays of the Members of either House on any question shall, at the Desire of one fifth of those Present, be entered on the Journal.

Neither House, during the Session of Congress, shall, without the Consent of the other, adjourn for more than three days, nor to any other Place than that in which the two Houses shall be sitting.

Section. 6. The Senators and Representatives shall receive a Compensation for their Services, to be ascertained by Law, and paid out of the Treasury of the United States. They shall in all Cases, except Treason, Felony and Breach of the Peace, be privileged from Arrest during their Attendance at the Session of their respective Houses, and in going to and returning from the same; and for any Speech or Debate in either House, they shall not be questioned in any other Place.

No Senator or Representative shall, during the Time for which he was elected, be appointed to any civil Office under the Authority of the United States, which shall have been created, or the Emoluments whereof shall have been encreased during such time; and no Person holding any Office under the United States, shall be a Member of either House during his Continuance in Office.

Section. 7. All Bills for raising Revenue shall originate in the House of Representatives; but the Senate may propose or concur with amendments as on other Bills.

Every Bill which shall have passed the House of Representatives and the Senate, shall, before it become a law, be presented to the President of the United States: If he approve he shall sign it, but if not he shall return it, with his Objections to that House in which it shall have originated, who shall enter the Objections at large on their Journal, and proceed to reconsider it. If after such Reconsideration two thirds of that House shall agree to pass the Bill, it shall be sent, together with the Objections, to the other House, by which it shall likewise be reconsidered, and if approved by two thirds of that House, it shall become a Law. But in all such Cases the Votes of both Houses shall be determined by Yeas and Nays, and the Names of the Persons voting for and against the Bill shall be entered on the Journal of each House respectively. If any Bill shall not be returned by the President within ten Days (Sundays excepted) after it shall have been presented to him, the Same shall be a Law, in like Manner as if he had signed it, unless the Congress by their Adjournment prevent its Return, in which Case it shall not be a Law.

Every Order, Resolution, or Vote to which the Concurrence of the Senate and House of Representatives may be necessary (except on a question of Adjournment) shall be presented to the President of the United States; and before the Same shall take Effect, shall be approved by him, or being disapproved by him, shall be repassed by two thirds of the Senate and House of Representatives, according to the Rules and Limitations prescribed in the Case of a Bill.

Section. 8. The Congress shall have Power To lay and collect Taxes, Duties, Imposts and Excises, to pay the Debts and provide for the common Defence and general Welfare of the United States; but all Duties, Imposts and Excises shall be uniform throughout the United States;

To borrow Money on the credit of the United States;

To regulate Commerce with foreign Nations, and among the several States, and with the Indian Tribes;

To establish an uniform Rule of Naturalization, and uniform Laws on the subject of Bankruptcies throughout the United States;

To coin Money, regulate the Value thereof, and of foreign Coin, and fix the Standard of Weights and Measures;

To provide for the Punishment of counterfeiting the Securities and current Coin of the United States;

To establish Post Offices and post Roads;

To promote the Progress of Science and useful Arts, by securing for limited Times to Authors and Inventors the exclusive Right to their respective Writings and Discoveries;

To constitute Tribunals inferior to the supreme Court;

To define and punish Piracies and Felonies committed on the high Seas, and Offences against the Law of Nations;

To declare War, grant Letters of Marque and Reprisal, and make Rules concerning Captures on Land and Water;

To raise and support Armies, but no Appropriation of Money to that Use shall be for a longer Term than two Years;

To provide and maintain a Navy;

To make Rules for the Government and Regulation of the land and naval Forces;

To provide for calling forth the Militia to execute the Laws of the Union, suppress Insurrections and repel Invasions;

To provide for organizing, arming, and disciplining, the Militia, and for governing such Part of them as may be employed in the Service of the United States, reserving to the States respectively, the Appointment of the Officers, and the Authority of training the Militia according to the discipline prescribed by Congress;

To exercise exclusive Legislation in all Cases whatsoever, over such District (not exceeding ten Miles square) as may, by Cession of Particular States, and the Acceptance of Congress, become the Seat of the Government of the United States, and to exercise like Authority over all Places purchased by the Consent of the Legislature of the State in which the Same shall be, for the Erection of Forts, Magazines, Arsenals, dock-Yards and other needful Buildings; _ And

To make all Laws which shall be necessary and proper for carrying into Execution the foregoing Powers and all other Powers vested by this Constitution in the Government of the United States, or in any Department or Officer thereof.

Section. 9. The Migration or Importation of such Persons as any of the States now existing shall think proper to admit, shall not be prohibited by the Congress prior to the Year one thousand eight hundred and eight, but a Tax or duty may be imposed on such Importation, not exceeding ten dollars for each Person.

The Privilege of the Writ of Habeas Corpus shall not be suspended, unless when in Cases of Rebellion or Invasion the public Safety may require it.

No Bill of Attainder or ex post facto Law shall be passed.

No Capitation, or other direct, Tax shall be laid, unless in Proportion to the Census of Enumeration herein before directed to be taken.

No Tax or Duty shall be laid on Articles exported from any State.

No Preference shall be given by any Regulation of Commerce or Revenue to the Ports of one State over those of another: nor shall Vessels bound to, or from, one State, be obliged to enter, clear or pay Duties in another.

No Money shall be drawn from the Treasury, but in Consequence of Appropriations made by Law; and a regular Statement and Account of the Receipts and Expenditures of all public Money shall be published from time to time.

No Title of Nobility shall be granted by the United States: And no Person holding any Office of Profit or Trust under them, shall, without the Consent of the Congress, accept of any present, Emolument, Office, or Title, of any kind whatever, from any King, Prince or foreign State.

Section. 10. No State shall enter into any Treaty, Alliance, or Confederation; grant Letters of Marque and Reprisal; coin Money; emit Bills of Credit; make any Thing but gold and silver Coin a Tender in Payment of Debts; pass any Bill of Attainder, ex post facto Law, or Law impairing the Obligation of Contracts, or grant any Title of Nobility.

No State shall, without the Consent of the Congress, lay any Imposts or Duties on Imports or Exports, except what may be absolutely necessary for executing it's inspection Laws: and the net Produce of all Duties and Imposts, laid by any State on Imports or Exports, shall be for the Use of the Treasury of the United States; and all such Laws shall be subject to the Revision and Controul of the Congress.

No State shall, without the Consent of Congress, lay any Duty of Tonnage, keep Troops, or Ships of War in time of Peace, enter into any Agreement or Compact with another State, or with a foreign Power, or engage in War, unless actually invaded, or in such imminent Danger as will not admit of delay.

Article. II.

Section. 1. The executive Power shall be vested in a President of the United States of America. He shall hold his Office during the Term of four Years, and, together with the Vice President, chosen for the same Term, be elected, as follows:

Each State shall appoint, in such Manner as the Legislature thereof may direct, a Number of Electors, equal to the whole Number of Senators and Representatives to which the State may be entitled in the Congress: but no Senator or Representative, or Person holding an Office of Trust or Profit under the United States, shall be appointed an Elector.

The Electors shall meet in their respective States, and vote by Ballot for two Persons, of whom one at least shall not be an Inhabitant of the same State with themselves. And they shall make a List of all the Persons voted for, and of the Number of Votes for each; which List they shall sign and certify, and transmit sealed to the Seat of the Government of the United States, directed to the President of the Senate. The President of the Senate shall, in the Presence of the Senate and House of Representatives, open all the Certificates, and the Votes shall then be counted. The Person having the greatest Number of Votes shall be the President, if such Number be a Majority of the whole Number of Electors appointed; and if there be more than one who have such Majority, and have an equal Number of Votes, then the House of Representatives shall immediately chuse by Ballot one of them for President; and if no Person have a Majority, then from the five highest on the List the said House shall in like Manner chuse the President. But in chusing the President, the Votes shall be taken by States, the Representatives from each State having one Vote; a quorum for this Purpose shall consist of a Member or Members from two thirds of the States, and a Majority of all the States shall be necessary to a Choice. In every Case, after the Choice of the President, the Person having the greatest Number of Votes of the Electors shall be the Vice President. But if there should remain two or more who have equal Votes, the Senate shall chuse from them by Ballot the Vice President.

The Congress may determine the Time of chusing the Electors, and the Day on which they shall give their Votes; which Day shall be the same throughout the United States.

No Person except a natural born Citizen, or a Citizen of the United States, at the time of the Adoption of this Constitution, shall be eligible to the Office of President; neither shall any person be eligible to that Office who shall not have attained to the Age of thirty five Years, and been fourteen Years a Resident within the United States.

In Case of the Removal of the President from Office, or of his Death, Resignation, or Inability to discharge the Powers and Duties of the said Office, the Same shall devolve on the Vice President, and the Congress may by Law provide for the Case of Removal, Death, Resignation or Inability, both of the President and Vice President, declaring what Officer shall then act as President, and such Officer shall act accordingly, until the Disability be removed, or a President shall be elected.

The President shall, at stated Times, receive for his Services, a Compensation, which shall neither be encreased nor diminished during the Period for which he shall have been elected, and he shall not receive within that Period any other Emolument from the United States, or any of them.

Before he enter on the Execution of his Office, he shall take the following Oath or Affirmation: –"I do solemnly swear (or affirm) that I will faithfully execute the Office of President of the United States, and will to the best of my Ability, preserve, protect and defend the Constitution of the United States."

Section. 2. The President shall be Commander in Chief of the Army and Navy of the United States, and of the Militia of the several States. when called into the actual Service of the United States; he may require the Opinion, in writing, of the principal Officer in each of the executive Departments, upon any Subject relating to the Duties of their respective Offices, and he shall have Power to Grant Reprieves and Pardons for Offences against the United States, except in Cases of Impeachment.

He shall have Power, by and with the Advice and Consent of the Senate, to make Treaties, provided two thirds of the Senators present concur; and he shall nominate, and by and with the Advice and Consent of the Senate, shall appoint Ambassadors, other public Ministers and Consuls, Judges of the supreme Court, and all other Officers of the United States, whose Appointments are not herein otherwise provided for, and which shall be established by Law: but the Congress may by Law vest the Appointment of such inferior Officers, as they think proper, in the President alone, in the Courts of Law, or in the Heads of Departments.

The President shall have Power to fill up all Vacancies that may happen during the Recess of the Senate, by granting Commissions which shall expire at the End of their next Session.

Section. 3. He shall from time to time give to the Congress Information on the State of the Union, and recommend to their Consideration such Measures as he shall judge necessary and expedient; he may, on extraordinary Occasions, convene both Houses, or either of them, and in Case of Disagreement between them, with Respect to the Time of Adjournment, he may adjourn them to such Time as he shall think proper; he shall receive Ambassadors and other public Ministers; he shall take Care that the Laws be faithfully executed, and shall Commission all the Officers of the United States.

Section. 4. The President, Vice President and all Civil Officers of the United States, shall be removed from Office on Impeachment for and Conviction of, Treason, Bribery, or other high Crimes and Misdemeanors.

Article. III.

Section. 1. The judicial Power of the United States, shall be vested in one supreme Court, and in such inferior Courts as the Congress may from time to time ordain and establish. The Judges, both of the supreme and inferior Courts, shall hold their Offices during good Behaviour, and shall, at stated Times, receive for their Services, a Compensation, which shall not be diminished during their Continuance in Office.

Section. 2. The judicial Power shall extend to all Cases, in Law and Equity, arising under this Constitution, the Laws of the United States, and Treaties made, or which shall be made, under their Authority; –to all Cases affecting Ambassadors, other public ministers and Consuls; –to all Cases of admiralty and maritime Jurisdiction; –to Controversies to which the United States shall be a Party; –to Controversies between two or more States; –between a State and Citizens of another State; –between Citizens of different States; –between Citizens of the same State claiming Lands under Grants of different States, and between a State, or the Citizens thereof, and foreign States, Citizens or Subjects.

In all Cases affecting Ambassadors, other public Ministers and Consuls, and those in which a State shall be Party, the supreme Court shall have original Jurisdiction. In all the other Cases before mentioned, the supreme Court shall have appellate Jurisdiction, both as to Law and Fact, with such Exceptions, and under such Regulations as the Congress shall make.

The Trial of all Crimes, except in Cases of Impeachment, shall be by Jury; and such Trial shall be held in the State where the said Crimes shall have been committed; but when not committed within any State, the Trial shall be at such Place or Places as the Congress may by Law have directed.

Section. 3. Treason against the United States, shall consist only in levying War against them, or in adhering to their Enemies, giving them Aid and Comfort. No Person shall be convicted of Treason unless on the Testimony of two Witnesses to the same overt Act, or on Confession in open Court.

The Congress shall have Power to declare the Punishment of Treason, but no Attainder of Treason shall work Corruption of Blood, or Forfeiture except during the Life of the Person attainted.

Article. IV.

Section. 1. Full Faith and Credit shall be given in each State to the public Acts, Records, and judicial Proceedings of every other State. And the Congress may by general Laws prescribe the Manner in which such Acts, Records and Proceedings shall be proved, and the Effect thereof.

Section. 2. The Citizens of each State shall be entitled to all Privileges and Immunities of Citizens in the several States.

A Person charged in any State with Treason, Felony, or other Crime, who shall flee from Justice, and be found in another State, shall on Demand of the executive Authority of the State from which he fled, be delivered up, to be removed to the State having Jurisdiction of the Crime.

No Person held to Service or Labour in one State, under the Laws thereof, escaping into another, shall, in Consequence of any Law or Regulation therein, be discharged from such Service or Labour, but shall be delivered up on Claim of the Party to whom such Service or Labour may be due.

Section. 3. New States may be admitted by the Congress into this Union; but no new State shall be formed or erected within the Jurisdiction of any other State; nor any State be formed by the Junction of two or more States, or Parts of States, without the Consent of the Legislatures of the States concerned as well as of the Congress.

The Congress shall have Power to dispose of and make all needful Rules and Regulations respecting the Territory or other Property belonging to the United States; and nothing in this Constitution shall be so construed as to Prejudice any Claims of the United States, or of any particular State.

Section. 4. The United States shall guarantee to every State in this Union a Republican Form of Government, and shall protect each of them against Invasion; and on Application of the Legislature, or of the Executive (when the Legislature cannot be convened) against domestic Violence.

Article. V.

The Congress, whenever two thirds of both Houses shall deem it necessary, shall propose Amendments to this Constitution, or, on the Application of the Legislatures of two thirds of the several States, shall call a Convention for proposing Amendments, which, in either Case, shall be valid to all Intents and Purposes, as Part of this Constitution, when ratified by the Legislatures of three fourths of the several States, or by Conventions in three fourths thereof, as the one or the other Mode of Ratification may be proposed by the Congress; Provided that no Amendment which may be made prior to the Year One thousand eight hundred and eight shall in any Manner affect the first and fourth Clauses in the Ninth Section of the first Article; and that no State, without its Consent, shall be deprived of it's equal Suffrage in the Senate.

Article. VI.

All Debts contracted and Engagements entered into, before the Adoption of this Constitution, shall be as valid against the United States under this Constitution, as under the Confederation.

This Constitution, and the Laws of the United States which shall be made in Pursuance thereof; and all Treaties made, or which shall be made, under the Authority of the United States, shall be the supreme Law of the Land; and the Judges in every State shall be bound thereby, any Thing in the Constitution or Laws of any state to the Contrary notwithstanding.

The Senators and Representatives before mentioned, and the Members of the several State Legislatures, and all executive and judicial Officers, both of the United States and of the several States, shall be bound by Oath or Affirmation, to support this Constitution; but no religious Test shall ever be required as a Qualification to any Office or public Trust under the United States.

Article. VII.

The Ratification of the Conventions of nine States, shall be sufficient for the Establishment of this Constitution between the States so ratifying the same.

Done in Convention by the Unanimous Consent of the States present the Seventeenth Day of September in the Year of our Lord one thousand seven hundred and Eighty seven and of the Independance of the United States of America the Twelfth. In witness whereof We have hereunto subscribed our Names.

Attest William Jackson Secretary

G° Washington
Presid^t and deputy from Virginia

Delaware   *Geo: Read   Gunning Bedford jun   John Dickinson
Richard Bassett   Jaco: Broom*
Maryland   *James McHenry   Dan of St. Thos. Jenifer
Danl. Carroll*
Virginia   *John Blair   James Madison Jr.*
North Carolina   *Wm. Blount   Richd. Dobbs Spaight
Hu Williamson*
South Carolina   *J. Rutledge   Charles Cotesworth Pinckney
Charles Pinckney   Pierce Butler*
Georgia   *William Few   Abr Baldwin*
New Hampshire   *John Langdon Nicholas Gilman*
Massachusetts   *Nathaniel Gorham   Rufus King*
Connecticut   *Wm. Saml. Johnson   Roger Sherman*
New York   *Alexander Hamilton*
New Jersey   *Wil: Livingston   David Brearley   Wm. Patterson
Jona: Dayton*
Pennsylvania   *B. Franklin   Thomas Mifflin   Robt. Morris
Geo. Clymer   Thos. FitzSimons   Jared ingersoll
James Wilson   Gouv Morris*

The Bill of Rights

[The following 10 amendments to the Constitution were approved in 1791. A further 17 amendments have been added since then – see following page.]

Amendment 1
Congress shall make no law respecting an establishment of religion, or prohibiting the free exercise thereof; or abridging the freedom of speech, or of the press; or the right of the people peaceably to assemble, and to petition the Government for a redress of grievances.

Amendment 2
A well regulated Militia, being necessary to the security of a free State, the right of the people to keep and bear Arms, shall not be infringed.

Amendment 3
No Soldier shall, in time of peace be quartered in any house, without the consent of the Owner, nor in time of war, but in a manner to be prescribed by law.

Amendment 4
The right of the people to be secure in their persons, houses, papers, and effects, against unreasonable searches and seizures, shall not be violated, and no Warrants shall issue, but upon probable cause, supported by Oath or affirmation, and particularly describing the place to be searched, and the persons or things to be seized.

Amendment 5
No person shall be held to answer for a capital, or otherwise infamous crime, unless on a presentment or indictment of a Grand Jury, except in cases arising in the land or naval forces, or in the Militia, when in actual service in time of War or public danger; nor shall any person be subject for the same offence to be twice put in jeopardy of life or limb; nor shall be compelled in any criminal case to be a witness against himself, nor be deprived of life, liberty, or property, without due process of law; nor shall private property be taken for public use, without just compensation.

Amendment 6
In all criminal prosecutions, the accused shall enjoy the right to a speedy and public trial, by an impartial jury of the State and district wherein the crime shall have been committed, which district shall have been previously ascertained by law, and to be informed of the nature and cause of the accusation; to be confronted with the witnesses against him; to have compulsory process for obtaining witnesses in his favor, and to have the Assistance of Counsel for his defence.

Amendment 7
In Suits at common law, where the value in controversy shall exceed twenty dollars, the right of trial by jury shall be preserved, and no fact tried by a jury, shall be otherwise re-examined in any Court of the United States, than according to the rules of the common law.

Amendment 8

Excessive bail shall not be required, nor excessive fines imposed, nor cruel and unusual punishments inflicted.

Amendment 9

The enumeration in the Constitution, of certain rights, shall not be construed to deny or disparage others retained by the people.

Amendment 10

The powers not delegated to the United States by the Constitution, nor prohibited by it to the States, are reserved to the States respectively, or to the people.

Some other important amendments since 1791:

Amendment 13 (ratified 1865)

Neither slavery nor involuntary servitude, except as a punishment for crime whereof the party shall have been duly convicted, shall exist within the United States, or any place subject to their jurisdiction. [...]

Amendment 14 (ratified 1868)

All persons born or naturalized in the United States, and subject to the jurisdiction thereof, are citizens of the United States and of the State wherein they reside. No State shall make or enforce any law which shall abridge the privileges or immunities of citizens of the United States; nor shall any State deprive any person of life, liberty, or property, without due process of law; nor deny to any person within its jurisdiction the equal protection of the laws. [...]

Amendment 15 (ratified 1870)

The right of citizens of the United States to vote shall not be denied or abridged by the United States or by any State on account of race, color, or previous condition of servitude. [...]

Amendment 18 (ratified 1919)

After one year from the ratification of this article the manufacture, sale, or transportation of intoxicating liquors within, the importation thereof into, or the exportation thereof from the United States and all territory subject to the jurisdiction thereof for beverage purposes is hereby prohibited. [...]

Amendment 19 (ratified 1920)

The right of citizens of the United States to vote shall not be denied or abridged by the United States or by any State on account of sex.
Congress shall have power to enforce this article by appropriate legislation.

Impeachment – a Definition

Impeachment is a proceeding in which accusations are brought by a legislative or executive branch of a government against civil officials or, in some cases, private citizens. Originally, it was a legislative function only, but the concept broadened after World War II. Accordingly, impeachment also may be brought by an executive body, or by a body exercising both executive and legislative functions.

Legally, the term "impeachment" applies only to the indictment. In popular usage, it embraces also the trial of the accused, conducted by the higher branch of a legislature, as in the United States and England; by a court, as in Belgium, France, India, and Italy; or by a combination of the two, as in some states of the United States. In most countries, impeachment is a device for removing civil officials (chiefs of state, cabinet ministers and judges). The modern institution did not originate until the latter part of the 14th century, in England, and it spread throughout the world. Today, impeachment clauses appear in the constitutions of many political systems throughout the world.

The writers of the US Constitution adopted the British procedure with modifications primarily designed to discourage the practice (then common in England) of using impeachment as an instrument of political warfare. The most conspicuous attempt in the United States to circumvent the intent of the founding fathers took place in 1868, when the Radical Republicans in control of the House of Representatives impeached President Andrew Johnson in an obvious attack on the federal system of checks and balances. The fullest expression of the radical view during the trial was Senator Charles Sumner's statement that "this proceeding is political in character ... with a political object". The one-vote acquittal of Johnson is generally held to have established beyond question that under the US Constitution impeachment is a *judicial*, rather than a *political*, process.

Six clauses in the federal Constitution embody the law: Article I, sections 2 and 3; Article II, section 2. The House indicts, the Senate tries, and the chief justice of the United States presides over the inquiry in case of impeachment of the president. A two-thirds vote of the senators present is required to convict. Punishment is limited to removal from office (with the acts of the accused still subject to criminal proceedings in the courts). Impeachable acts are "Treason, Bribery, or other high Crimes and Misdemeanors".

These provisions have proved a fertile source of vexing questions. What are "high Crimes and Misdemeanors"? Partly because of these ambiguities, but chiefly because the trial ties up the Senate for as much as six weeks, impeachment has taken place infrequently at the national level. Repeated attempts in Congress to simplify impeachment or to establish a special court for the removal of judges have fallen before the enduring conviction that the present procedure, however cumbersome, is a necessary element of the system of checks and balances.

Adapted from an article by Milton Lomask, author of *Andrew Johnson: President on Trial*. For the full article, see the following website:
http://gi.grolier.com/presidents/ea/side/impeach.htm!

Donkeys and Elephants

A famous 19th century cartoonist, Thomas Nast, first drew the Democratic Party as a donkey and the Republican Party as an elephant in 1874, in separate cartoons. The symbols caught on immediately. A contemporary described the Democratic party as being "like a mule – without pride of ancestry or hope of posterity".

The elephant was defined in 1904 thus: "Among the elephant's known characteristics are cleverness and unwieldiness. He is an animal easy to control until he is aroused; but when frightened or stirred up, he becomes absolutely unmanageable. Here we have all the characteristics of the Republican vote."

These two symbols have been used by political cartoonists ever since.

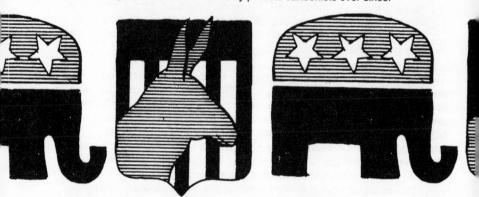

Artist's Acknowledgements

Thanks to Duncan Heath for the preparation of the text, and to Simon Flynn for chasing up pictures of some of America's lesser-known political worthies. Thanks also to various members of my family: to my wife Sarah and my sons William and Timothy for their timely assistance with picture research and for turning the ancient craft of paste-up work into something of a cottage industry. Above all, thanks to my brother Robert for his tireless attention to the exacting task of typesetting and page layout and for his advice, patience and generosity.

About the authors

Patrick Brogan came to Washington as correspondent of the London *Times* in 1973. Previously he was Paris correspondent for *The Times*, and reported from many parts of the world. He has worked for the *Daily News* in New York, and been correspondent for *The Independent* and *The Observer*, as well as writing for *The Washington Post* and *Time Magazine*. He is the author of a number of books, including *World Conflicts*, a study of armed conflicts since 1945, and *Eastern Europe, 1945 to 1989*.

Chris Garratt has for many years produced *The Guardian*'s weekly BIFF strip. He has illustrated several previous titles in this series, including *Keynes*, *Postmodernism*, *Ethics* and *Descartes*. He teaches part-time in the Faculty of Arts and Education at the University of Plymouth, and runs the Blue Lagoon dance band.

Index

HB 6 FF